Fodor's
25 Best

LONDON

Contents

INTRODUCING LONDON   4

An overview of the city and its history, as well as top tips on making the most of your stay.

TOP 25   12

We've pulled together all the Top 25 must-see sights and experiences in London.

MORE TO SEE   64

Even more options of great places to visit if you have plenty of time to spend in the city, whether it's in the city center or farther afield.

CITY TOURS   80

We've broken the city into areas, with recommended tours in each one to help you get the best from your visit.

SHOP   118

Discover some of London's best shops and what they have to offer, from local produce to fashion and books.

KEY TO SYMBOLS

➕ Map reference to the accompanying pull-out map

✉ Address

☎ Telephone number

🕐 Opening/closing times

🍴 Restaurant or café

Ⓜ Nearest subway (Metro) station

🚌 Nearest bus route

🚃 Nearest rail station

ENTERTAINMENT 128

Whether you're after a cultural fix or just want a place to relax with a drink after a hard day's sightseeing, we've made the best choices for you.

EAT 140

Uncover great dining experiences, from a quick bite at lunch to top-notch evening meals.

SLEEP 152

We've brought together the best hotels in the city, whatever budget you're on.

NEED TO KNOW 160

The practical information you need to make your trip run smoothly.

PULL-OUT MAP

The fold-out map with this book is a comprehensive street plan of the city. We've given grid references within the book for each sight and listing.

🛥 Nearest riverboat or ferry stop
♿ Facilities for visitors with disabilities
ℹ Tourist information
❓ Other practical information

🎟 Admission charges:
  Expensive (over £10),
  Moderate (£5–£10) and
  Inexpensive (under £5)
▷ Further information

Introducing London

Prepare for London to challenge your expectations. The dynamic British capital's traditions, from Savile Row outfitters to parading Horse Guards, thrive alongside a cutting-edge cultural calendar, arts venues, museums and world-class restaurants.

London buzzes with energy as whole areas of the capital have been revitalized. Spectacular modern architecture soars above ancient buildings. The cleaning of St. Paul's Cathedral revealed its true glory; Tate Modern provides great spaces in which to enjoy contemporary art; and the Millennium Footbridge, spanning the Thames between the two sights, gives a modern edge to one of the world's best panoramic city views. Along the river, restaurants fill renovated warehouses, and gardens, museums, markets and theater and arts complexes have regenerated the South Bank.

In the redeveloped Docklands, the old Port of London is now a glittering world of skyscrapers, dominated by innovative Canary Wharf. Building for the 2012 Olympic Games has transformed districts in the East End and these are now some of the most vibrant places in the city to explore and discover (▷ 6–7).

Amid all this change, the greatness of London's 2,000 years of history has not been quashed. Visitors can still roam around one of Britain's finest medieval forts, the Tower of London, or visit a real royal home, Buckingham Palace. Equally, you can picnic in one of the royal parks or take a boat ride along the Thames to evoke times when the river was the backbone of London and its great port.

Londoners themselves—while appreciating their good-value theaters, free museums, great buildings and wealth of traditions—are likely to moan about just about everything else, from the high cost of property and living to the Congestion Charge and over-crowded public transport. Yet, in truth, they know they are living in one of the world's most vibrant cities. London, the artistic, political and financial capital of Britain, is hard to beat. Everything you could ever want is here; it is up to you to take it and enjoy it.

FACTS AND FIGURES

- Greater London covers 1,584sq km (612sq miles). With a population of more than 8.53 million, it is Europe's largest city.
- London is the most culturally diverse city in Britain and more than 300 languages are spoken in the capital.
- London is the only city to have hosted the Summer Olympics three times (1908, 1948 and 2012).

CITY WITHIN A CITY

The City of London covers about 2.5sq km (1sq mile) and is Europe's largest central business and financial district. Referred to by Londoners either as "The City" or "The Square Mile," it has a daily working population that swells to over 300,000. The City has its own administration and police force and every year elects its own Lord Mayor.

DOWN UNDER

The London Underground (the Tube) is the oldest underground rail network in the world. The first line opened in 1863: 6km (4 miles) between Paddington and Farringdon Street on the Metropolitan Line. Today the Tube carries more than 1.3 billion passengers per year on 11 lines covering 402km (249 miles) of track and serving 270 stations.

BEATING THE COSTS

London is expensive, so start by working out what is free. Top of the list are most major museums and galleries, the parks, monuments such as churches, and a variety of entertainment including lunch-time concerts and other events. To cut unavoidable costs, buy a Travelcard (Oyster card) and perhaps the London sightseeing pass (▷ 167).

Look East

London's East End has shaken off its notoriety to become a hub of cutting-edge fashion, food, art and music. It's still gritty, but therein lies its attraction, and you will find plenty of places to tempt you to stop awhile, eat, browse and explore.

A Long History

East of the medieval walled City of London and north of the River Thames, the East End has long housed immigrant and refugee communities, from the Huguenot silk weavers who settled in Spitalfields in the late 17th century to the Bangladeshis who began arriving in the 1970s. Each wave of new arrivals added to the local culture and some buildings reflect the changing demographics: on Brick Lane, a chapel built by Huguenots in 1742 was first adapted for use by Methodists, then became the Spitalfields Great Synagogue and is now the Great London Mosque (Jamme Masjid).

Poverty and appalling living conditions attracted social reformers in the 19th century, leading to the formation of workers' associations and unions. As well as being a byword for urban deprivation, in the early 20th century the East End became known as a hotbed of radicalism, while its docks and industry made it a target for heavy bombing during World War II. Regeneration began in the 1990s with the development of Canary Wharf, a new Docklands business and financial district. More recently, East London has benefited from the 2012 Olympic and Paralympic Games, with thousands of new homes being built in a green environment. The Queen Elizabeth Olympic Park hosts concerts and festivals and the sports facilities are superb.

Cutting-edge Cool

Once Whitechapel, Spitalfields, Hoxton and the area around Brick Lane in Shoreditch (nearest tube Aldgate East) were associated

Clockwise from top: Unusual housewares for sale on Columbia Road; enjoying the sunshine in the Allen Gardens; crowds of shoppers on Brick Lane, famous for

with slums and crime. Today a young, edgy and arty crowd have made these districts cool, with galleries and warehouse art exhibitions, cutting-edge fashion, trendy clubs and bars, an indie music scene, festivals, events and eye-popping street art.

In this foodie melting pot with cheap eats galore, try Korean fried chicken, steamed buns and *kimchi* in Shoreditch, Turkish grills in Dalston, Punjabi curry feasts and Vietnamese street food in Whitechapel, vegetarian and vegan fare in Walthamstow or the pie and mash and jellied eels that have been traditional East End staples since the 1800s.

Vibrant Markets

Head east on a Sunday and browse the vibrant markets—Columbia Road's flower and plant market (nearest tube Old Street) is an East End institution and a visual treat. Lining the street are little shops where new meets vintage and innovative crafts sit alongside friendly cafés.

Brick Lane is famous for vintage fashion and alternative designers, secondhand furnishings, arts, crafts and kitsch collectibles. The Old Truman Brewery at 91 Brick Lane is a good place to start. Here you'll find the Sunday Upmarket featuring established designers and artists; Homegrown, a showcase for independent designers and makers; Backyard and Vintage Markets; and the Boiler House Food Hall, where international specialties are displayed under high ceilings and the brewery's landmark chimney.

Lively street performers entertain the Brick Lane crowds, and the ethnic eateries that line this long street span everything from Jewish bagel and salt-beef shops to authentic Bangladeshi curry houses—of which there are so many that the area has become known as Banglatown and is often referred to as London's "curry hub."

its vintage fashion stores, kitsch collectibles and curry houses; the Aquatics Centre in the Queen Elizabeth Olympic Park; Jamme Masjid mosque on Brick Lane

Top Tips For...

These great suggestions will help you tailor your ideal visit to London, no matter how you choose to spend your time. Each sight or listing has a fuller write-up elsewhere in the book.

Serious Retail Therapy

Start on the ground floor of **Harrods** (▷ 124–125) and work your way up.
Spend a whole day in **Harvey Nichols** (▷ 125) or **Selfridges** (▷ 127).
Search **Liberty** (▷ 126) for accessories.
Make a weekend foray into the five markets in **Camden Markets** (▷ 123).
Tempt your taste buds at **Borough Market's** (▷ 66–67) wonderful array of organic and artisan food stalls.

A Meal with a View

Book a table at the **Portrait Restaurant** on top of the National Portrait Gallery (▷ 149).
Rendezvous at the Kitchen and Bar on level 6 of the **Tate Modern** (▷ 151).
Go to Canary Wharf to eat at the waterside gastropub **The Gun** (▷ 147).
Take in the panoramic London views from atop the riverside **Oxo Tower** (▷ 149).
Eat stylishly amid trees and flamingos at the rooftop **Babylon** (▷ 144).

A Breath of Fresh Air

Roam **Hampstead Heath** (▷ 77) and visit **Kenwood House** (▷ 77).
Climb high in **Greenwich Park** (▷ 20–21) to enjoy London views.
Enjoy botanical riches from around the world at **Kew Gardens** (▷ 77).
Go boating in **Regent's Park** (▷ 73) and visit the **Zoo** (▷ 75).
Do the great central London royal park walk: through **St. James's** (▷ 42–43), **Green Park** (▷ 70) and **Hyde Park** (▷ 71), then **Kensington Gardens** (▷ 26–27).

Clockwise from top: Harrods—the ultimate department store; the Great Court of the British Museum; crowds gather to watch the Changing the Guard ceremony at

After Dark

Try **The Jazz Café** (▷ 135) or the **Bull's Head**, Barnes (▷ 133–134) for quality jazz, or **The Pheasantry**, Chelsea (▷ 137) for fun cabaret. See a play at **Shakespeare's Globe** (▷ 139) or enjoy a classical music concert at the **Cadogan Hall** (▷ 134).

Hear cutting-edge house, electronica and techno at the superclub **Fabric** (▷ 135) or head south of the river to the **Ministry of Sound** (▷ 136) for high-energy clubbing.

Watching the Bank Balance

Opt for bed-and-breakfast at **The Beaver** (▷ 156) or the **Morgan Hotel** (▷ 158). Head to **Gaby's Deli** (▷ 146) on Charing Cross Road for hearty, no-nonsense food. Go to a free concert in a church such as **St. James's**, **Piccadilly** (▷ 73). Visit a free museum such as the **British Museum** (▷ 16–17).

Peeking Inside Londoners' Homes

Clarence House (▷ 68), to see where Prince Charles entertains.
Sir John Soane's two houses (▷ 74), filled with his antiquities.
Handel House (▷ 70), the famous composer's home for 36 years.
Buckingham Palace (▷ 18–19), the Queen's London home.
Apsley House (▷ 66), the perfect place to discover more about the Duke of Wellington, hero of the Battle of Waterloo.

Keeping the Kids Happy

Handle objects at the hands-on tables in the **British Museum** (▷ 16–17). Climb the stairs to the top of **St. Paul's Cathedral** (▷ 45). Go boating in **Regent's Park** (▷ 73). See an Astronaut's moon capsule in the **Science Museum** (▷ 47).

Buckingham Palace; the Making the Modern World gallery at the Science Museum; time out in Green Park; the 19th-century Palm House at Kew Gardens

Timeline

1042 Edward the Confessor becomes king, making London the capital of England and Westminster his home; builds the abbey church of St. Peter.

1066 The Norman king, William the Conqueror, defeats King Harold at the Battle of Hastings; begins the Tower of London.

1485 Tudor rule begins, ending in 1603 with the death of Elizabeth I.

1533 Henry VIII breaks with Rome to marry Anne Boleyn; establishes the Church of England.

1649 Charles I is executed; the Commonwealth (1649–53) and Protectorate (1653–59) govern England until Charles II is restored to the throne in 1660.

1666 The Great Fire of London.

1759 The British Museum, London's first public museum, opens.

1851 The Great Exhibition is held in Hyde Park.

1863 World's first urban underground train service opens. In 1890 the first deep-dug train runs (known as the Tube).

1939–45 Blitz bombings destroy a third of the City of London and much of the docks.

EARLY LONDON

- Emperor Claudius invades Britain in AD43; a deep-water port, Londinium, is soon established.
- In AD200 the Romans put a wall around Londinium, now capital of Britannia Superior; they withdraw in 410.

THE GREAT FIRE

The fire broke out at a baker's near Pudding Lane on the night of 2 September 1666. Raging for four days and nights, it destroyed four-fifths of the City of London and 13,200 homes. Sir Christopher Wren became the grand architect of the subsequent rebuilding of the city.

The London's Burning exhibit in the Museum of London shows the devastation caused by the fire

An attack by Luftwaffe bombers during the Blitz

1960s The Beatles, Carnaby Street and the King's Road help create "swinging London."

1981 Regeneration and development of London Docklands begins.

1994 First Eurostar trains link London and Paris through the Channel Tunnel.

2002 Queen Elizabeth II celebrates her Golden Jubilee.

2005 London 7/7 bombings kill 52 people and injure many more.

2011 Prince William marries Catherine Middleton.

2012 The city hosts the Olympic Games and marks the Queen's Diamond Jubilee.

2013 Birth of Prince George, third in line to the throne.

2015 Birth of Princess Charlotte of Cambridge, fourth in line to the throne.

2016 The UK votes to leave the European Union; results show that London voted to remain.

2017 London and Manchester hit by terrorist attacks but residents remain defiant and the cities open for business; Grenfell Tower blaze is one of the worst in UK history.

2018 Expected completion of Crossrail, with around 100km (62 miles) of track linking 40 stations to transform London's transport system.

GROWING CITY

● During the 16th century, London was Europe's fastest-growing city; its population rose from 75,000 to 200,000.
● By 1750, London was Europe's biggest and wealthiest city, with a population of about 700,000.
● London's population continued to grow, from around 1 million in 1800 to 6.5 million by 1900, peaking during World War II at 9 million.
● The city's population is currently more than 8 million and rising.

The Great Exhibition of 1851

The Eurostar terminal at St. Pancras station

Top 25

This section contains the must-see Top 25 sights and experiences in London. They are listed alphabetically, and numbered so you can locate them on the inside front cover.

1. Banqueting House	**14**
2. British Museum	**16**
3. Buckingham Palace	**18**
4. Greenwich	**20**
5. Houses of Parliament	**22**
6. Imperial War Museum	**24**
7. Kensington Palace and Gardens	**26**
8. Knightsbridge Shopping	**28**
9. London Eye	**30**
10. Museum of London	**32**
11. National Gallery	**34**
12. National Portrait Gallery	**36**
13. Natural History Museum	**38**
14. Portobello Road Market	**40**
15. St. James's Park	**42**
16. St. Paul's Cathedral	**44**
17. Science Museum	**46**
18. Shakespeare's Globe	**48**
19. Somerset House	**50**
20. Tate Britain	**52**
21. Tate Modern	**54**
22. Thames River Cruise	**56**
23. Tower of London	**58**
24. Victoria and Albert Museum	**60**
25. Westminster Abbey	**62**

TOP 25

⭐ 1 Banqueting House

- Rubens ceiling
- Allegory of James I between Peace and Plenty
- Allegory of the birth and coronation of Charles I
- Weathercock put on the roof by James II
- Vaulted undercroft, a drinking den for James I
- Whitehall river terrace in Embankment Gardens
- Video and self-guided audio tour

It is chilling to imagine Charles I calmly crossing the park from St. James's Palace to be beheaded outside the glorious hall built by his father. The magnificent ceiling was painted for Charles by Flemish artist Peter Paul Rubens.

Magnificent rooms This, all that remains of Whitehall Palace, was London's first building to be coated in smooth white Portland stone. Designed by Inigo Jones and built between 1619 and 1622, it marked the beginning of James I's dream to replace the original sprawling Tudor palace with a 2,000-room Palladian masterpiece. In fact, it was only the banqueting hall that was built. Inside, the King hosted small parties in the crypt and presided over lavish court ceremonies upstairs.

Clockwise from far left: The main hall, with ceiling paintings by Rubens; the elegant neoclassical exterior; a bust of Charles I, who was executed outside the Banqueting House in 1649; Rubens's nine allegorical ceiling paintings, which depict the unification of Scotland and England

Rubens ceiling The stunning ceiling was commissioned by James's son, Charles I. Painted between 1634 and 1636 by Peter Paul Rubens, the panels celebrate James I, who was also James VI of Scotland. Nine allegorical paintings show the unification of Scotland and England and the joyous benefits of wise rule. Rubens waited two years for his £3,000 fee.

The demise The palace has had its fair share of bad luck. Cardinal Thomas Wolsey lived so ostentatiously that he fell from Henry VIII's grace. Henry made it his, and his successors', main London royal home. Charles I was beheaded here on 30 January 1649, and William III suffered from the dank river air. A fire in 1698 wiped out the Tudor building, leaving only the Banqueting House.

THE BASICS

hrp.org.uk

🔲 K6

✉ Whitehall, SW1

☎ 020 3166 6155

🕐 Check website or call to confirm opening times

🚇 Westminster, Charing Cross, Embankment

♿ Good (call ahead of visit to confirm arrangements)

✋ Moderate

❓ Occasional lunchtime and evening concerts

HIGHLIGHTS

- Enlightenment Gallery
- Oriental antiquities
- African galleries
- Rosetta Stone
- Living and Dying Gallery
- Parthenon sculptures
- Assyrian and Egyptian rooms
- Norman Foster's Great Court redevelopment

TIPS

- Pick up a plan in the Great Court and choose just a few rooms to explore.
- Take an Eye Opener tour.
- Do the Hands-On object handling.
- Rent an audio guide.

The collection here is truly breathtaking, with a wealth of ancient treasures, among them bronzes from the Indian Chola dynasty and the lion-filled reliefs that once lined the walls of an Assyrian palace.

Physician founder Sir Hans Sloane, after whom Sloane Square is named, was a fashionable London physician, "interested in the whole of human knowledge" and an avid collector of everything from plants to prints. When he died in 1753, aged 92, he left his collection of more than 71,000 objects to the nation on condition that it was given a permanent home. Thus began the British Museum, opened in 1759 in a 17th-century mansion, Britain's first public museum and now its largest, covering 5.5ha (13.5 acres), with eight million objects.

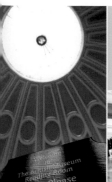

Clockwise from far left: The Queen Elizabeth II Great Court, designed by Foster + Partners; the historic circular Reading Room, at the heart of the Great Court; exhibits in the museum's Egyptian collection; the museum's imposing main entrance

Expansion George II, George III and George IV added to Sloane's collection, as did other monarchs. Their gifts, combined with the Townley and Parthenon sculptures, burst the building's seams, and so architect Robert Smirke designed a new museum, completed by his son, Sydney, in 1857. Even so, with booty from expeditions and excavations pouring in, the natural history collections moved to South Kensington (▷ 38–39). When the British Library (▷ 67) moved to St. Pancras in 1998, the Great Court was redeveloped and the King's Library transformed into a gallery on the Enlightenment.

Starting to explore Head to the glass-and-steel-roofed Great Court, a magnificent space with an education center, lecture theaters, seminar rooms and cafés, to get your bearings.

THE BASICS

britishmuseum.org

🔲 J3

✉ Great Russell Street, WC1 (another entrance in Montague Place)

☎ 020 7323 8181

🕐 Galleries: Sun–Thu 10–5.30, Fri 10–8.30. Great Court: Sun–Thu 9–6, Fri 9–8.30

🍴 Restaurant, cafés

Ⓜ Holborn, Tottenham Court Road

♿ Very good

💷 Free, except for some temporary exhibitions

❓ Full educational schedule

HIGHLIGHTS

- The Queen's Gallery
- Changing the Guard
- State Coach, Royal Mews
- Nash's facade, Quadrangle
- Gobelin tapestries in the Guard Room
- Throne Room
- Van Dyck's portrait of Charles I and family

TIPS

- To avoid the lines, book a timed ticket in advance.
- Visit the quality royal souvenir shops.

Of the capital's houses now open to visitors, the Queen's London home is perhaps the most fascinating. Where else can you see a living sovereign's private art collection, drawing rooms and horse harnesses?

Yet another palace British royals have had homes across London over the years, moving from Westminster to Whitehall to Kensington and St. James's, and finally to Buckingham Palace. It was George III who bought the prime-site mansion in 1761 as a gift for his new bride, the 17-year-old Queen Charlotte, leaving St. James's Palace as the official royal residence.

Grand improvements King George IV and his architect John Nash made extravagant changes using Bath stone, later covered up by Edward

Clockwise from far left: Buckingham Palace is the London home of the British sovereign—the red, gold and blue Royal Standard is raised when the Queen is in residence; visitors at the palace gates; the Grand Staircase, designed by John Nash; the Mall, the ceremonial route to the palace

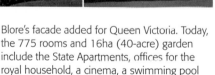

Blore's facade added for Queen Victoria. Today, the 775 rooms and 16ha (40-acre) garden include the State Apartments, offices for the royal household, a cinema, a swimming pool and the Queen's private rooms.

Open house The Queen inherited the world's finest private art collection. The Queen's Gallery, completely refurbished for her Golden Jubilee in 2002, exhibits some of her treasures in changing exhibitions. In the Royal Mews, John Nash's stables house gleaming fairy-tale coaches, harnesses and other apparel used for royal ceremonies. Don't miss the Buckingham Palace Summer Opening, when visitors can wander through the grand State Rooms resplendent with gold, pictures, porcelain, tapestries and thrones, and enjoy the gardens.

THE BASICS

royal.uk
royalcollection.org.uk
🔲 G7
✉ Buckingham Gate, SW1
☎ Tickets and information 0303 123 7334
🕐 Queen's Gallery daily 10–5.30, last admission 4.15. Royal Mews:
1 Feb–25 Mar Mon–Sat 10–4; 26 Mar–31 Oct daily 10–5; Nov Mon–Sat 10–4, last admission 45 min before closing. Various seasonal closures may apply, so check in advance. State Rooms, Buckingham Palace: 5–30 Aug daily 9.30–7.30; 1–24 Sep daily 9.30–6.30, last admission 2 hours 30 min before closing
🚇 Victoria, Hyde Park Corner, Green Park
🚉 Victoria
♿ Excellent
💷 Expensive
❓ No photography

HIGHLIGHTS

- *Captain Augustus Keppel* by Sir Joshua Reynolds (Queen's House)
- Maritime equipment at the National Maritime Museum
- The Painted Hall, where Nelson's body lay in state after the Battle of Trafalgar
- Winter stargazing at the Royal Observatory

A UNESCO World Heritage Site, this historic district is a great day out, enthralling children and adults with science, sea stories and an excellent art collection. The town itself has a market, restaurants and a park.

Old Royal Naval College and the *Cutty Sark* Stop first at the *Cutty Sark*, once one of the fastest tea clippers in the world. Ravaged by fire in 2007, it took five years to restore. Continue into the main quadrangle of the Old Royal Naval College. With your back to the Thames, the remarkable Painted Hall, notable for its spectacular ceiling, is on the right.

Art and maritime heritage At the foot of Greenwich Park, the Queen's House and National Maritime Museum stand adjacent to

Clockwise from far left: The Royal Observatory, designed by Sir Christopher Wren; the Greenwich Meridian, the point chosen as 0° longitude; the Cutty Sark's figurehead; the Galvanic Magnetic Clock on the Greenwich Meridian, from which time around the world is measured

THE BASICS

visitgreenwich.org.uk
➕ See map ▷ 115
✉ Greenwich, SE10
🍴 Restaurants and cafés
🚇 DLR Greenwich, Cutty Sark
🚉 Greenwich, Maze Hill
⛴ From Westminster
Old Royal Naval College
ornc.org
☎ 020 8269 4747
🕐 Grounds daily 8am–11pm; Painted Hall, Chapel and Discover Greenwich Visitor Centre daily 10–5, last admission 30 min before closing. Talks and guided walks available
The Queen's House, Royal Observatory, Planetarium, National Maritime Museum and Cutty Sark
rmg.co.uk
☎ 020 8858 4422
🕐 Daily 10–5; last admission 30 min before closing; Cutty Sark last admission 4.15

each other. The Queen's House is beautifully proportioned, but the real surprise is the outstanding art collection inside. The National Maritime Museum is crammed with hands-on exhibits that answer pressing questions such as why the sea is salty. Boats on display range from small dinghies to the *Miss Britain III*, the first powerboat to top 100mph. Don't miss the navigational equipment and Asian treasures in the East India Company gallery.

Astronomical delights Inside Sir Christopher Wren's cramped Observatory, small galleries explain how time is measured. But the new astronomy galleries of the Planetarium next door merit much more time; they're modern, engaging and exciting, without oversimplifying the bigger questions about the universe.

5 Houses of Parliament

HIGHLIGHTS

● View of the building from Westminster Bridge
● Big Ben
● Summer tours
● St. Stephen's Hall
● Westminster Hall
● State opening of Parliament
● Central Lobby
● Afternoon tea after a tour (advance booking essential)

Britain is governed from this landmark building alongside the River Thames. For many visitors, its clock tower and Big Ben chiming the hour symbolize London. Interesting tours reveal its architecture, traditions and the workings of government.

Powerhouse for crown and state William the Conqueror made Westminster his seat of rule to watch over the London merchants. It was soon the heart of government for England, then for Britain, then for a globe-encircling empire. It was also the principal home of the monarchs until Henry VIII moved to Whitehall. Here the foundations of Parliament were laid according to Edward I's Model Parliament of 1295: a combination of elected citizens, lords and clergy. This developed into the House of

Clockwise from top left: A nighttime view of the Houses of Parliament from the South Bank; Thomas Thornycroft's early 20th-century bronze of Boadicea, by Westminster Bridge; Big Ben and the London Eye; Central Lobby, a meeting place between the House of Commons and the House of Lords

Commons (elected Members of Parliament) and the House of Lords (unelected senior members of State and Church). Henry VIII's Reformation Parliament of 1529–36 ended Church domination of Parliament and made the Commons more powerful than the Lords.

Fit for an empire Having survived the Catholic conspiracy to blow up Parliament on 5 November 1605, most of the buildings were destroyed by a fire in 1834. Kingdom and empire needed a new headquarters. With Charles Barry's plans and A.W. Pugin's detailed design, a masterpiece of Victorian Gothic was created. Behind the facade, the Lords is on the left and the Commons on the right. If Parliament is in session, there is a flag on Victoria Tower or, at night, a light on Big Ben.

THE BASICS

parliament.uk

✚ K8

✉ Westminster, SW1

☎ 020 7219 3000; Commons 020 7219 4272; Lords 020 7219 3107; tickets 020 7219 4114

◑ Visits to House of Commons public gallery when house is sitting: Mon 2.30–10.30, Tue–Wed 11.30–7.30, Thu 9.30–5.30, Fri 9.30–3. Tours during summer recess (late Jul–early Sep) and Sat all year 9–4.15 (timed tickets). Audio and guided tours in seven languages. UK citizens can arrange tours at other times through their MP

Ⓠ Westminster

🚉 Waterloo

👜 Parliament free; tours expensive

❓ Airport-style security screening in operation

HIGHLIGHTS

● First World War galleries
● Atrium: Witnesses to War
● Turning Points
1934–1945
● Family in Wartime
exhibition
● Western Front trench
● The Holocaust Exhibition
● The Lord Ashcroft
Gallery: Extraordinary
Heroes
● Curiosities of War
● Modern conflicts:
Kosovo, Iraq and
Afghanistan

Covering conflicts and their impact from World War I to the present day, this museum offers a thoughtful look at what life was like for soldiers and citizens, using personal objects, military might and testimonies from those who fought and those facing the challenges of life at home.

Extending its remit Originally conceived as a museum to collect and display material relating to the Great War, the Imperial War Museum opened to the public in the Crystal Palace in 1920. It moved to its present location, in what had been the Bethlem Royal Hospital (known as "Bedlam"), in 1936. By 1953 its remit had been extended to include all military operations in which Britain or the Commonwealth have been involved since 1914.

Clockwise from left: The impressive entrance and grounds of the Imperial War Museum; admiring the naval guns outside the museum; detail on an "Ole Bill" bus from World War I; tanks on display in the large exhibits gallery

New galleries A £40-million refurbishment resulted in the spectacular, much-enlarged First World War galleries in 2014, together with a redesign of the dramatic, four-story-high atrium, created by the innovative architecture and design team at Foster + Partners. The displays include a Spitfire, Harrier Jump Jet, V-1 "doodle-bug" and V-2 bombs suspended above field guns, and a T34 tank.

Created to coincide with the centenary of World War I, the galleries feature more than 1,300 original objects, including letters and diaries from the front line, interactive multi-media displays that give insight into life in the trenches and at home, and help visitors understand the war and its global impact. Among the objects on display are weapons, uniforms, keepsakes and trinkets, photographs and art.

THE BASICS

iwm.org.uk

➕ M8

✉ Lambeth Road, SE1

☎ 020 7416 5000

🕐 Daily 10–6, last admission 5.30

🍴 Café daily 10–5.30. Tea Room peak times and school holidays

🚇 Lambeth North, Waterloo

🚆 Waterloo, Elephant and Castle

♿ Excellent

💷 Free; charge for some temporary exhibitions

❓ Full education schedules, talks and events

HIGHLIGHTS

- The King's grand staircase
- The Queen's state apartments
- Wind dial, King's Gallery
- Luminous Lace light piece
- Princess Victoria's dolls' house
- Royal dresses
- Tea in the Orangery
- The Sunken Garden

It's difficult not to be charmed by this royal residence with its grand state apartments, galleries and sunken garden—truly a fitting home for modern royals the Duke and Duchess of Cambridge and Prince Harry.

Perfect location The year William III became king in 1689, he and his wife Mary bought a mansion in tiny Kensington village. William suffered with asthma, so the cleaner air here suited him, while the couple also wanted to be well placed for London socializing and country living. Sir Christopher Wren and Nicholas Hawksmoor were brought in to remodel and enlarge the house. Despite the small rooms, George I introduced palatial grandeur with Colen Campbell's staircase and state rooms. Queen Anne added the Orangery (the architect

Clockwise from far left: A view of the palace from Dial Walk in Kensington Gardens; a statue commemorating William III, the palace's first royal resident; George Frampton's famed statue of Peter Pan in Kensington Gardens; the Orangery; the peaceful Italian Garden, a Victorian addition

was Hawksmoor and the woodcarver was Grinling Gibbons) and annexed a chunk of royal Hyde Park, a trick repeated by George II's wife, Queen Caroline, who created the Round Pond and Long Water to complete the 110ha (272-acre) Kensington Gardens. Today, trees are the backdrop for sculptures (such as George Frampton's fairy-tale *Peter Pan*, ▷ 72), monuments and contemporary exhibitions at the lakeside Serpentine Gallery and Sackler Gallery.

New look A £12-million project has opened up previously unseen areas of the palace, including fine state apartments and landscaped public gardens. The routes focus on different historical eras and figures, including Diana, Princess of Wales, and Queen Victoria, whose story is told in her own words.

THE BASICS

hrp.org.uk
serpentinegalleries.org
✚ A6
✉ Kensington Gardens, W8
☎ 020 3166 6000
☎ Serpentine Gallery 020 7402 6075
◷ Mar–Oct daily 10–6; Nov–Feb daily 10–4; last admission 1 hour before closing. Serpentine Galleries Tue–Sun 10–6
🍴 Café, Orangery (▷ 149)
🚇 High Street Kensington, Queensway
♿ Good
💰 Expensive. Serpentine free
❓ Personalized tours by expert Explainers

HIGHLIGHTS

● Food halls at Harrods
● Designer fashion at Harvey Nichols
● Boutiques on Walton Street

TIPS

● In Harrods, check out the day's events, shows and demos.
● If you need a special outfit, no staff are more helpful than those at Harvey Nichols.
● If it rains, stay put in Harrods and visit the spa.

Knightsbridge is London's smartest and most expensive neighborhood, with real estate, shops and price tags to match. It's the place for some serious retail therapy.

Stylish shops As you leave the Underground station (Sloane Street exit) you'll see Harvey Nichols (▷ 125), London's most fashionable department store. On emerging from Harvey Nichols, head back toward the Underground and continue along Brompton Road. Opposite is a huge Burberry store, known for its tan-and-gray check designs. On the left, as you walk toward the canopied shopfront of Harrods (▷ 124–125), is Swarovski, with its window displays of crystal jewelry. Leave Harrods by the Hans Road exit and you'll see luxury lingerie store Rigby & Peller across the street.

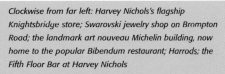

Clockwise from far left: Harvey Nichols's flagship Knightsbridge store; Swarovski jewelry shop on Brompton Road; the landmark art nouveau Michelin building, now home to the popular Bibendum restaurant; Harrods; the Fifth Floor Bar at Harvey Nichols

Even more stylish shops Return to Brompton Road and pass leather store Mulberry, before turning left into Beauchamp Place for smart restaurants, designer fashion and the Map House, with its precious maps and engravings. At the end of Beauchamp Place, turn right into attractive Walton Street, lined with interior design, jewelry and children's clothes shops. With Chanel to your right across Brompton Road, turn left into Sloane Avenue by the iconic Michelin building famed for its design, decor and Bibendum restaurant (▷ 145). The flagship Conran Shop, selling contemporary design for the home, is on the right, with fashion from Joseph for Men on the left. Continue down Sloane Avenue to reach the King's Road or turn left for Sloane Square, home to Peter Jones, the department store (▷ 126).

THE BASICS

🔒 D7–E7

✉ Knightsbridge

🍴 Harvey Nichols' 5th floor is dedicated to food. Go to Harrods for elegant dining and macaroons. The Berkeley Hotel, Wilton Place, tel 020 7235 6000, serves Pret-à-Portea, a fashionista afternoon tea (daily)

🚇 Knightsbridge

HIGHLIGHTS

● Panoramic views across the city in every direction
● On a clear day you can see for 40km (25 miles)
● Spotting landmarks along the Thames
● Aerial view of the Palace of Westminster

TIPS

● It is best to book ahead, although not essential.
● Evening riders enjoy the London lights.
● Tickets include access to the 4-D Experience, a 3-D film with special effects.

Attracting four million visitors a year, London's most visible attraction, soaring 135m (443ft) above the South Bank of the Thames, affords spectacular city views.

Riding high Passengers ride in one of the 32 capsules that rotate smoothly through 360 degrees in a slow-moving 30-minute flight. Each capsule is fully enclosed and comfortably holds 25 people. Because the capsules are secured on the outside of the wheel (rather than hung from it like a Ferris wheel), views through the large glass windows are totally unobstructed. Passengers can walk freely inside the capsules, which are kept level by a motor-ized motion-stability system—although seating is provided. Each capsule is in touch with the ground via camera and radio links. The wheel is

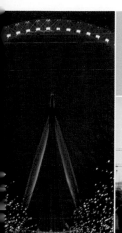

Clockwise from far left: Opened in 2000, the Eye quickly became an established part of the South Bank's landscape; the Eye at night; the glass capsules, attached to the outside of the wheel, offer unobstructed views; an aerial view of the Palace of Westminster at dusk

in constant motion, revolving continuously at 0.26m (0.85ft) per second, a quarter of the average walking speed, enabling passengers to walk straight on and off the moving capsules. After dark, the trees lining the approach to the London Eye are bathed in magical blue lights, while the boarding platform appears to float on a cloud of more blue light.

Revolutionary design Conceived by David Marks and Julia Barfield to celebrate the millennium, the Eye represents the turning of the century and is a universal and ancient symbol of regeneration. It took seven years and the expertise of people from five European countries for their design to be realized. The Eye is on the riverside Thames Path, which runs east all the way to the Thames Barrier.

THE BASICS

londoneye.com

⊞ L7

✉ Riverside Gardens, next to County Hall, SE1

🕐 Daily 10am to mid- or late evening depending on time of year. Check website for details

🍴 Riverfront cafés

Ⓔ Waterloo, Westminster, Embankment, Charing Cross

Ⓡ Waterloo

♿ Very good. Boarding ramp available for wheel-chair users

💰 Expensive

HIGHLIGHTS

- London Before London gallery
- Hoard of 43 gold Roman coins
- Spitalfields Woman (Roman)
- Viking grave
- The lavish, late-18th-century Fanshawe dress
- Model of Tudor London
- Pleasure Gardens
- The London 2012 Olympics Cauldron gallery

A visit here is easily the best way to cruise through London's 2,000 years of history, pausing to see a Roman shoe or the Lord Mayor's state coach, or to peek through a Victorian shop window; and it is even built on the West Gate of London's Roman fort.

A museum for London This is the world's largest and most comprehensive city museum, opened in 1976 in a building by Powell and Moya. The collection combines the old Guildhall Museum's City antiquities with the London Museum's costumes and other culturally related objects. The continuous building work and redevelopment in the City since the 1980s, allied with increased awareness about conservation, has ensured a steady flow of archaeological finds into the collection.

Clockwise from left: The lavish 18th-century Lord Mayor's state coach on display at the museum; a window to the city's past—the original museum building, built in the 1970s; coins from the second century AD, part of the impressive Roman exhibit

ANTONINUS PIUS
Emperor AD138–61

A museum about London The building is, appropriately, in the barbican of the Roman fort, and the rooms are laid out chronologically to keep the story clear. The London Before London gallery follows the story of prehistoric Londoners before Roman settlement. One of the most impressive galleries is Roman London, which covers the period from the founding of Londinium in about AD50 until AD410, when the Roman army quit Britain. The Expanding City chronicles the Great Fire of 1666 to the 1850s, an era of wealth, power and global influence. People make a city, so in every room it is Londoners who are really telling the story, whether it is through Roman ceramics or Tudor clothes. A major redevelopment has resulted in superb displays and a mesmerizing re-creation of the 18th-century Vauxhall Pleasure Gardens.

THE BASICS

museumoflondon.org.uk
✚ P3
✉ 150 London Wall, EC2
☎ 020 7001 9844
🕐 Daily 10–6; galleries close 5.40
🍴 Cafés, restaurant
Ⓜ Barbican, St. Paul's
🚆 Liverpool Street, City Thameslink, Farringdon
♿ Excellent
💷 Free; prices vary for temporary exhibitions
❓ Full education schedule; audio tour

HIGHLIGHTS

- *Virgin Enthroned*, Cenni di Peppi (aka Cimabue)
- Cartoon, Leonardo da Vinci
- *Pope Julius II*, Raphael
- *The Arnolfini Wedding*, van Eyck
- Equestrian portrait of Charles I by van Dyck
- *The Haywain*, John Constable
- *Madonna of the Pinks*, Raphael
- *The Archers*, Henry Raeburn
- *Sunflowers*, van Gogh
- *Mr and Mrs William Hallett*, Gainsborough
- *La Pointe de la Hève*, Monet
- Restored entrance lobby and galleries

Britain's premier art gallery holds some of the world's most famous paintings and it's free to visit, so you can drop in for a few minutes' peace in front of *The Haywain* or Rubens's ravishing *Samson and Delilah*.

Quality collection Founded in 1824 with just 38 pictures, the National Gallery now has more than 2,300 paintings, all on show. Spread throughout William Wilkins' neoclassical building and the Sainsbury Wing extension, they provide a high-quality, concise panorama of European painting from Giotto to Cézanne.

Free from the start Unusual for a national painting collection, the nucleus is not royal but the collection of John Julius Angerstein, a self-made financier. From the start it was open to

Clockwise from far left: The gallery's impressive neoclassical facade, fronting Trafalgar Square; one of the elegant galleries in the East Wing; a detail of Vincent van Gogh's 1888 painting Sunflowers; the East Wing of the National Gallery; the exterior of the museum

all, free of charge, and provided a wide spectrum of British painting within a European context—aims that are still maintained today. However, there may be a charge for the temporary exhibitions in the Sainsbury Wing.

A first visit To take advantage of the rich artistic panorama, choose a room from each of the four chronologically arranged sections. Early paintings by Duccio di Buoninsegna, Jan van Eyck, Piero della Francesca and others fill the Sainsbury Wing. The West Wing has 16th-century pictures, including Michelangelo's *Entombment*, while the North Wing is devoted to 17th-century artists such as van Dyck, Rubens, Rembrandt and painters of the Dutch school. The East Wing runs from Chardin through Gainsborough to Matisse and Picasso.

THE BASICS

nationalgallery.org.uk

➕ J6

✉ Trafalgar Square, WC2

☎ 020 7747 2885

🕐 Sat–Thu 10–6, Fri 10–9

🍴 Restaurant, café

🚇 Charing Cross, Leicester Square

🚃 Charing Cross

♿ Excellent

🖐 Free

❓ Guided tours (free daily 11.30 and 2.30, also Fri 7pm), lectures, films, audio guide, interactive screens. Free 10-minute talks (Mon–Fri 4pm), free lunchtime talks (days vary, 1pm)

HIGHLIGHTS

● *Self-portrait with Barbara Hepworth*, Ben Nicholson
● *Richard II*
● The Tudor Galleries
● *Queen Victoria*, Sir George Hayter
● *The Brontë Sisters*, by Branwell Brontë
● An unfinished sketch of Jane Austen (*c.*1810) by her sister, Cassandra

TIP

● Join the late shift for free live music, DJs, talks and events every Thu and Fri 6–9pm.

It's always fascinating to see what someone famous looked like and how they chose to be painted. The National Portrait Gallery has iconic images from the Tudors right up to the present day.

British record Founded in 1856 to collect portraits of the great and good in British life, and so inspire others to greatness, this is now the most comprehensive collection of its kind in the world, comprising watercolors, oil paintings, caricatures, silhouettes and photographs.

Start at the top The galleries, incorporating the Ondaatje Wing, are arranged chronologically, starting on the second floor—reached by stairs or elevator. Tudor monarchs kick off a visual *Who's Who* of British history that moves

Clockwise from far left: The main entrance to the National Portrait Gallery; the Tudor Galleries; portraits and busts from the Regency period in the Weldon Galleries; an 1834 portrait of the Brontë sisters by their brother, Branwell (right) and Jenny Lind (left); mosaic at the museum entrance

through inventors, merchants, explorers and empire builders to modern politicians. Here you'll find Isambard Kingdom Brunel, Robert Clive and Warren Hastings of India, Winston Churchill and Margaret Thatcher. There is Chaucer in his floppy hat, Kipling at his desk and A.A. Milne with his engaging tales, Christopher Robin and Winnie-the-Pooh on his knee. Lesser-known sitters also merit a close look, such as the 18th-century portrait of the extensive Sharp family, who formed an orchestra and played at Fulham every Sunday.

Modern times Among the famous portraits from history, you may also spot a number of more familiar, contemporary faces, such as the footballer David Beckham, Sir Paul McCartney and Madonna.

THE BASICS

npg.org.uk

J5

St. Martin's Place, WC2

020 7306 0055

Sat–Wed 10–6, Thu–Fri 10–9

Café, rooftop restaurant

Leicester Square, Charing Cross

Charing Cross

Good

Free except for special exhibitions

Lectures, events, explorer touchscreens

13 Natural History Museum

- Giant Earth sculpture
- Dinosaur skeletons
- Fossilized frogs
- The Vault, a gallery of crystals, gems and meteorites
- Restless Surface Gallery
- Tank Room in the Darwin Centre

TIPS

- Use the side entrance on Exhibition Road.
- The museum is huge: Plan your visit carefully.

The museum building looks like a Romanesque cathedral and is wittily decorated with a zoo of animals to match its contents—extant animals on the west side, extinct ones on the east side.

Two museums in one Overflowing the British Museum, the Life Galleries were moved here in 1881. They tell the story of life on earth. The story of the Earth itself is told in the Earth Galleries, beginning with a 300-million-year-old fossil of a fern. The Darwin Centre uses technology to make the most of the museum's 70 million objects and make the work of its 300 or so scientists accessible worldwide. Take the glass lift to its futuristic Cocoon building, then wend your way down its sloping walkways, taking in the exciting insect and plant displays.

Clockwise from far left: The Whale Hall; the escalator leading to the Red Zone, where galleries explore the nature of the Earth; insect specimens on display at Cocoon, part of the Darwin Centre; the original 1880 Waterhouse Building

Follow the zone The skeleton of a blue whale, the largest creature on Earth, seems to dive through the heart of the great Hintze Hall. This gateway to the galleries was given a spectacular makeover in 2017. Color coded zones help you plan your visit. In the Red Zone, dramatic sculptures and a giant metallic globe lead to galleries revealing how the planet has evolved and the effects of man on nature. Exhibits in the Green Zone include birds, minerals and creepy crawlies. The Blue Zone celebrates the amazing diversity of our planet, from humans and mammals to fish and dinosaurs. Don't miss the Images of Nature gallery, at the end of the Blue Zone, which houses a stunning collection of art inspired by nature. The superb Darwin Centre and quiet wildlife garden occupy the Orange Zone.

THE BASICS

nhm.ac.uk

🚇 B8

✉ Cromwell Road, SW7; also entrance on Exhibition Road

☎ 020 7942 5000

🕐 Daily 10–5.50, last admission 5.30

🍴 Meals, snacks, deli café, picnic areas

🚇 South Kensington

♿ Excellent

💶 Free; charge for some temporary exhibitions

❓ Regular tours, lectures, films, workshops

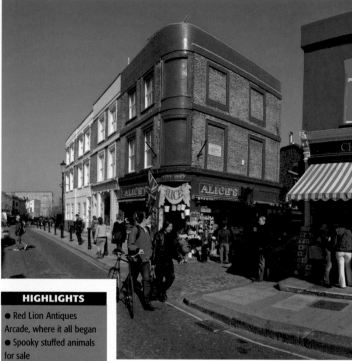

HIGHLIGHTS

● Red Lion Antiques Arcade, where it all began
● Spooky stuffed animals for sale
● The clocks and watches in Admiral Vernon Arcade
● Arts and crafts and art deco in the Rogers Arcade

TIPS

● Saturday is by far the best day, when the antiques dealers set up stalls in the street.
● No price is totally fixed; bargain hard.
● It is true that the early bird finds the best prices.
● Grab a sidewalk café table for gourmet coffee, gelato and great cakes.

Spend a Saturday wandering down Portobello Road, peering at the stalls and dipping into the shops behind them to seek out a special piece of china, a fascinating piece of glass or a pretty piece of jewelry.

Portobello Road Originally a lane leading down to Porto Bello Farm, named after the town of Porto Bello in Panama, captured by the British from the Spanish in 1739, this road has been a market site for more than a century. Travelers traded horses and herbs here in the 1870s, but the antiques dealers arrived only in the late 1940s. Today, Portobello Road Market claims to be the world's largest antiques market. It is really a series of markets that spill into surrounding streets where almost everything imaginable is sold.

Clockwise from left: Antiques arcades and galleries line Portobello Road; the Saturday-morning antiques market, when antiques traders and bargain-hunters crowd the area, sees Portobello Road at its busiest; fruit and vegetables are sold in the market's lower reaches

More than just stalls Starting at the top, there are the established specialist antiques shops for maps, silver, medals and collectibles, where bargains are few. Don't miss the arcades, packed with dealers in tiny kiosks. Farther down, where the stalls begin, the stock is more varied and you can join locals in the pubs and cafés to discuss values and possible purchases. Here you'll find antique clothes, records and china next to contemporary ceramics and jewelry. Explore the byroads, too.

For something different After the vegetable and organic food stalls, go under the Westway flyover and find restorative cafés. The tone changes here; look for funky bric-a-brac, cutting-edge street fashion, vintage clothes and even secondhand bicycles.

THE BASICS

portobelloroad.co.uk;
shopportobello.co.uk
+ See map ▷ 114
✉ Market office:
72 Tavistock Road, W11
☎ 020 7727 7684
🕐 Mon–Wed 9–6,
Thu 9–1, Fri–Sat 9–7
🚇 Notting Hill Gate,
Ladbroke Grove

HIGHLIGHTS

- Springtime daffodils
- Whitehall views from the lake bridge
- Feeding the pelicans, daily 2.30–3
- Views to Buckingham Palace
- Exotic plants in the tropical border

TIPS

- Inn the Park café opens early and closes late.
- The park is the perfect setting for summer picnics.
- Cyclists are welcome in the royal parks.

Drop in to St. James's Park to picnic and laze on a deckchair, try spotting palaces across the duck-filled lake or follow part of the Diana, Princess of Wales Memorial Walk.

Royal heart St. James's Park is the oldest and most royal of London's eight royal parks, surrounded by the Palace of Westminster, St. James's Palace, Buckingham Palace and the remains of Whitehall Palace. Kings and their courtiers have been frolicking here since 1532, when Henry VIII laid out a deer park in what was then marshy water meadow and built a hunting lodge that became St. James's Palace. Elizabeth I held fetes here, and in the early 17th century James I began the menagerie, including crocodiles and an elephant who drank a gallon of wine daily.

Left to right: With Buckingham Palace at its western end and the Houses of Parliament within easy reach, the park is a popular retreat for visitors; a drinking fountain; early spring, when the daffodils are in bloom, is one of the best times to visit

French order In the mid-17th century, Charles II, influenced by Versailles, near Paris, redesigned the park to include a canal, Birdcage Walk (where he kept aviaries) and the graveled Mall, where he played pell mell, a game similar to croquet. George IV, helped by John Nash and influenced by Humphrey Repton, softened the formal French lines into the English style in the 19th century, making this 37ha (93-acre) park of blossoming shrubs and curving paths popular with romantics.

Nature As the park is an important migration point and breeding area for birds, two full-time ornithologists look after up to 1,000 birds from more than 45 species. Pelicans live on Duck Island, a tradition begun when the Russian Ambassador gave some to Charles II in 1664.

THE BASICS

royalparks.org.uk

🚻 J7

✉ The Mall, SW1

☎ 0300 061 2350

🕐 Daily 5am–midnight

🍴 Inn the Park (▷ 147)

🚇 St. James's Park, Green Park, Westminster

🚉 Victoria

♿ Very good

💷 Free

❓ Changing the Guard (on Horse Guards Parade). Bird talks and guided walks

HIGHLIGHTS

- Sung evensong
- Frescoes and mosaics
- Wren's Great Model in the Triforium (upstairs)
- Triple-layered dome weighing 76,000 tons
- Jean Tijou's wrought-iron sanctuary gates
- Wellington's memorial
- *Light of the World*, Holman Hunt
- The view across London
- Wren's epitaph under the dome

To slip into St. Paul's for evensong, and sit gazing up at the mosaics as the choir's voices soar, is to enjoy a moment of absolute peace and beauty. Go early or late to avoid the crowds.

Wren's London After the restoration of the monarchy in 1660, artistic patronage bloomed under Charles II. Following the Great Fire of London in 1666, which destroyed four-fifths of the City, Christopher Wren took main stage as King's Surveyor-General. The spires and steeples of his 51 churches, of which 23 still stand, surrounded his masterpiece, St. Paul's.

The fourth St. Paul's This cathedral church for the diocese of London was founded in AD604 by King Ethelbert of Kent. The first three

Clockwise from far left: The view of St. Paul's Cathedral from Festival Gardens; the interior of the magnificent dome, decorated with frescoes by Sir James Thornhill; the choir stalls and high altar; St. Paul's before the Fire of London in 1666; architect Sir Christopher Wren

The West View of St. Paul's Cathedral before the Fire of London

churches burned down. Wren's, built in stone and paid for with a special coal tax, was the first English cathedral built by a single architect, the only one with a dome, and the only one in the English baroque style. A £40-million cleaning-and-repair project marked the cathedral's 300th anniversary in 2010. Statues and memorials of Britain's famous crowd the interior and crypt—heroes Wellington and Nelson, artists Turner and Reynolds, as well as Wren himself.

The climb The 528 steps to the Golden Gallery at the top are worth the effort. Shallow steps rise to the Whispering Gallery for views of Sir James Thornhill's dome, decorated with frescoes and 19th-century mosaics. For virtual access to the dome, visit Oculus, a 270-degree film experience in the crypt.

THE BASICS

stpauls.co.uk

🔒 N4

✉ Ludgate Hill, EC4

☎ 020 7246 8350

🕐 Mon–Sat 8.30–4.30, last admission 4, Sun for worship only. Daily services range from morning prayer to choral evensong

🍴 Restaurant, café

Ⓢ St. Paul's

🚆 City Thameslink

♿ Very good

💷 Expensive

❓ Multimedia, audio and guided tours included; organ recitals

17 Science Museum

HIGHLIGHTS

● Demonstrations
● Mathematics: The Winton Gallery
● Wonderlab's interactive exhibits and shows
● The glass bridge in the Challenge of Materials
● Pattern Pod, the hands-on gallery for children aged five to eight
● Atmosphere Gallery
● Puffing Billy
● 18th-century watches and clocks

Even if you are no scientist, it's thrilling to understand how a plane flies, how Newton's reflecting telescope worked or how we receive satellite television. You'll find the answers using interactive exhibits. This is science at its most accessible.

Industry and science Opened in 1857, this museum comes closest to fulfilling Prince Albert's educational aims when he founded the South Kensington Museums after the Great Exhibition of 1851. Its full title is the National Museum of Science and Industry. Over the seven floors, which contain more than 60 collections, the story of human industry, discovery and invention is recounted through various tools and products, from exquisite Georgian cabinets to a satellite launcher.

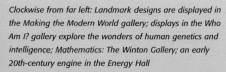
Clockwise from far left: Landmark designs are displayed in the Making the Modern World gallery; displays in the Who Am I? gallery explore the wonders of human genetics and intelligence; Mathematics: The Winton Gallery; an early 20th-century engine in the Energy Hall

Science made fun See how vital everyday objects were invented and then developed for use in Making the Modern World; find out what makes you smarter than a chimp in Who Am I?; and get involved in the very latest scientific hot topics in Antenna. The galleries vary from rooms of beautiful 18th-century objects to an astronaut's moon capsule and in-depth explanations of abstract concepts. Historic steam engines feature in the Energy Hall, while overhead walkways in the Flight gallery bring you close to some amazing aeroplanes. Discover how mathematics connects to every aspect of our lives in the stunning new Zaha Hadid-designed Mathematics: The Winton Gallery, with its flowing, organic shapes, or let the children loose in the high-tech, interactive Wonderlab: The Statoil Gallery.

THE BASICS

sciencemuseum.org.uk
🚇 C8
✉ Exhibition Road, SW7
🕐 Daily 10–6, last admission 5.15 (check website for late opening dates)
🍴 Restaurants, cafés, picnic area in basement
Ⓠ South Kensington
♿ Excellent (tel helpline 020 7942 4000)
🎟 Free; IMAX and temporary exhibitions expensive; Wonderlab moderate
❓ Guided tours, films, demonstrations, historic characters, workshops

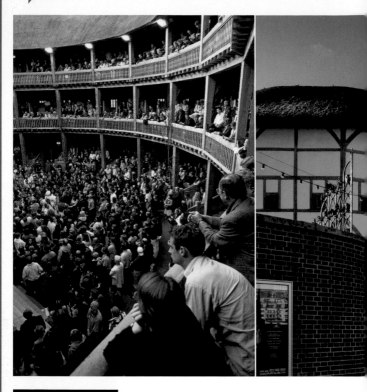

HIGHLIGHTS

- Guided tour storytellers
- Attending a performance
- Interactive displays
- Costume collection

TIP

- Tours and performances take place in all weathers, so dress appropriately.

A faithful reconstruction of the Bard's open-air theater, this South Bank landmark presents many of his plays, as well as work by his contemporaries and new writers.

One man's vision From his first visit to London in 1949, actor and director Sam Wanamaker dreamed of re-creating Shakespeare's 16th-century Globe theater as close as possible to its original site by the Thames at Bankside. Several decades and a long struggle later, the theater opened in 1997 with a production of *Henry V*.

Tradition to the core Constructed of English oak with mortise-and-tenon joints, lime plaster and water-reed thatch roof (the first permitted since the Great Fire of London in 1666), the building techniques used were painstakingly

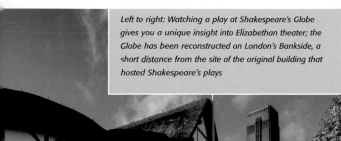

Left to right: Watching a play at Shakespeare's Globe gives you a unique insight into Elizabethan theater; the Globe has been reconstructed on London's Bankside, a short distance from the site of the original building that hosted Shakespeare's plays

accurate. Its thrust stage projects into a large circular yard surrounded by three tiers of simple benches (cushions can be hired) for 857 people. Only the seating area and stage are covered, so the 700 "groundlings" standing in the yard below the stage swelter in the heat and get very wet when it rains. An exhibition beneath the theater tells its history and explores the London Shakespeare would have known.

New theater A £7.5-million indoor Jacobean theater, the Sam Wanamaker Playhouse, has created an intimate, year-round theatrical experience, quite different from that of the Globe. Performing the plays of Shakespeare and his contemporaries in the surroundings for which they were originally intended, it seats 340 people and is predominantly lit by candles.

THE BASICS

shakespearesglobe.com

✚ P6

✉ 21 New Globe Walk, SE1

☎ Exhibition and tour office 020 7902 1500 Theatre Box Office 020 7401 9919

⏰ Exhibition daily 9–5; tours daily 9.30–5, every 30 min. Main stage performance season mid-Apr to mid-Oct

🍴 Restaurant, bar, café

Ⓜ Blackfriars, Mansion House, London Bridge, Southwark

🚆 London Bridge

🚢 Bankside Pier

♿ Good access; information line tel 020 7902 1409

💷 Expensive (includes guided theater tour and exhibition audio guide)

❓ Temporary exhibitions, full educational schedule

HIGHLIGHTS

- The Courtauld Collection
- The Fridart Collection
- *A Bar at the Folies-Bergère*, Manet
- Paintings by Rubens
- *The Trinity with Saints*, Botticelli

Somerset House has been transformed from a lavish but forgotten building into a riverside palace. Spend some time here and enjoy French Impressionist masterpieces, summer concerts and dancing fountains.

Palatial home A majestic triple-arch gateway leads from the Strand into Sir William Chambers' English Palladian government offices (1776–86). The Courtauld Collection is housed in rooms lavishly decorated for the Royal Academy, before its move to Piccadilly. Ahead, the great courtyard has fountains, a theater, an ice-rink and café tables, according to the season. A superb fine dining restaurant on the summer terrace, with sweeping Thames views, is a seasonal treat. Changing exhibitions are held in the Embankment Galleries.

Clockwise from far left: The courtyard of Somerset House; artistic treasures on display in the Courtauld Gallery; the Courtauld's lavishly decorated rooms, which were originally used by the Royal Academy; the elegant staircase leading to the upper floors of the Courtauld Gallery

Courtauld Gallery Industrialist Samuel Courtauld's collection of French Impressionist and Postimpressionist paintings, with works by Renoir, Cézanne, van Gogh, Manet, Seurat and Gauguin, are on display. There are also 18th-century portraits by Goya and Gainsborough, canvases and sketches by Rubens, works by Botticelli and Tintoretto and an important Gothic and medieval collection. Twentieth-century highlights include works by Matisse, Dufy, Kandinsky and the Bloomsbury group.

Drawings, prints and sculpture The excellent collection of prints includes works by Dürer, Michelangelo and Leonardo da Vinci, while the sculpture collection spans antiquity to the 20th century. The decorative arts are represented by fine Islamic ceramics and metalwork.

THE BASICS

somersethouse.org.uk

➕ L5

✉ Somerset House, Strand, WC2

☎ 020 7845 4600

🕐 Daily 10–6; extended hours for Courtyard, River Terrace and restaurant. Ice rink mid-Nov to mid-Jan

🍴 Cafés, restaurants

🚇 Temple

🚉 Blackfriars, Charing Cross, Waterloo

♿ Excellent

💷 Somerset House free; Courtauld Gallery moderate

❓ Free guided tours of Somerset House Tue 12.45, 2.15, Thu 1.15, 2.45, Sat 12.15, 1.15, 2.15 and 3.15. Tickets available from 10.30am from the information desk in the Seaman's Hall, South Building

HIGHLIGHTS

- The Clore Gallery
- A Thomas Gainsborough portrait
- *Flatford Mill*, Constable
- A William Blake vision
- A William Hogarth caricature
- A Barbara Hepworth stone or wood sculpture
- A work on paper by David Hockney
- *The Opening of Waterloo Bridge*, Constable
- Temporary exhibitions
- The Tate-to-Tate ferry

With galleries rich in Gainsborough portraits, Turner landscapes, Hepworth sculptures and more, this is an intimate social history of Britain told by its artists.

The Gallery The Tate Gallery was opened in 1897, named after the millionaire Henry Tate, who paid for the core building and donated his Victorian pictures to it. The national collection, renamed Tate Britain after the modern art collection was moved to Tate Modern (▷ 54–55), remain in the original building on Millbank.

The Millbank Project This is a 20-year program of building works designed to transform the gallery. Launched in 2010, the first phase has upgraded the Millbank Entrance, Rotunda and some of the galleries.

Clockwise from far left: The imposing Millbank entrance to Tate Britain; paintings on display in the gallery; the rotunda dome, a masterpiece of Victorian architecture; the Turner Collection, the largest collection of works by J.M.W. Turner in the world, is housed in the modern Clore Gallery

British art The galleries are helpfully divided into four chronological suites. You can follow the visual story of British art from 1500 until the present day. Although paintings, sculptures, installations and works in other media are changed regularly, you may well see van Dyck's lavish portraits of the 17th-century British aristocracy, William Hogarth's prints and richly colored Pre-Raphaelite canvases. Do not miss the great Turner collection housed in the adjoining Clore Gallery.

Turner Prize Britain's most prestigious and controversial prize to celebrate young British talent is run by the Tate and awarded each autumn. Founded in 1984, winners have included Damien Hirst, Grayson Perry, Duncan Campbell and Chris Ofili.

THE BASICS

tate.org.uk

✚ J9

✉ Millbank, SW1; entrances on Millbank and Atterbury Street

☎ 020 7887 8888

🕐 Daily 10–6, last admission 5.15

🍽 Restaurant, café

Ⓜ Pimlico, Vauxhall, Westminster

🚆 Vauxhall, Victoria

♿ Very good

✋ Free except for special exhibitions

❓ Full education schedule; audio tours

- The dramatic Turbine Hall, the heart of the old power station
- Installation art
- Interactive digital projects
- The award-winning multimedia guides (small charge)

TIP

- The Tate Boat travels between Tate Modern and Tate Britain every 40 minutes during opening times.

Tate Modern is the most visited modern art gallery in the world, its collection filling the magnificent rejuvenated spaces of George Gilbert Scott's vast Bankside Power Station.

World-class building Winning an international competition, Swiss architects Herzog & de Meuron were commissioned to convert the brick building. They worked with the size of the power station to create a contemporary gallery space, most notably the majestic Turbine Hall, standing 25m (85ft) from floor to glass-paned ceiling. Outside, the graceful pedestrian Millennium Bridge spans the Thames.

Art works The most influential artists of the 20th century are displayed within the spacious galleries, including Picasso, Matisse, Dalí,

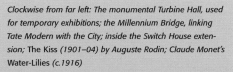

Clockwise from far left: The monumental Turbine Hall, used for temporary exhibitions; the Millennium Bridge, linking Tate Modern with the City; inside the Switch House extension; The Kiss (1901–04) *by Auguste Rodin; Claude Monet's* Water-Lilies (c.1916)

Duchamp, Rodin, Klee and Warhol—as well as British artists such as Bacon, Hepworth, Hockney and Nicholson. Just as much importance is given to performance art, films and installations, many of which you can interact with, down in the Tanks.

Transformation A revitalized gallery opened in 2016. The striking new 10-story Switch House extension includes three new gallery levels and a panoramic roof terrace, more than doubling the exhibition space. Accordingly, the gallery's artworks have been completely rehung, show-casing more than 300 artists from around 50 countries. A huge sculpture of a tree created by acclaimed Chinese artist Ai Weiwei, 7m (22ft) tall, was put on display in the Turbine Hall to mark the relaunch.

THE BASICS

tate.org.uk

🚇 N6

✉ Bankside, SE1

☎ 020 7887 8888

🕐 Sun–Thu 10–6, Fri–Sat 10–10

🍽 Cafés, restaurant

🚇 Blackfriars, Southwark

🚆 Blackfriars, London Bridge

♿ Very good

💷 Free; charge for some special exhibitions

❓ Full educational schedule. Choice of free daily audio tours

HIGHLIGHTS

- Lambeth Palace
- Houses of Parliament
- London Eye
- St. Paul's Cathedral
- Tower Bridge
- Tower of London
- Thames Barrier

TIPS

- Shop around for the best deals.
- The full circular tour takes about 1 hour.
- Take a jacket as London weather changes quickly.

A cruise along the Thames is a leisurely way to see the city. It gives a new perspective to London's development and history, which is inextricably linked with this great river.

Wonderful sights Many companies run river cruises and water-buses on the Thames. One particularly good stretch is from Westminster Pier in an easterly direction, which takes in a host of sights. This marks the point where the river enters central London and becomes a working highway, until recently lined with shipping, docks and warehouses. At this point the Thames flows between Lambeth Palace and the Houses of Parliament (▷ 22–23) and then past the London Eye (▷ 30–31) and the Southbank Centre, making a northern loop past the Victoria Embankment and toward the

Clockwise from top left: A view over the Thames to St. Paul's Cathedral and the high-rises of the City; amphibious craft (DUKWs) provide tours with a difference (see panel, ▷ 167); the landmark Tower Bridge; Big Ben and the Houses of Parliament; the Thames Flood Barrier

Millennium Bridge, which links St. Paul's Cathedral (▷ 44–45) and Tate Modern (▷ 54–55).

Great bridges Beyond the Globe (▷ 48–49) and Southwark Cathedral (▷ 74) the river reaches London Bridge, the modern crossing that replaced the 1831 version, itself replacing its arched medieval predecessor. The next crossing is Tower Bridge, designed to allow tall ships passage between the city and the sea. On the north bank is the Tower of London (▷ 58–59), placed strategically to protect the port.

Modern versus maritime From here the river passes the redeveloped Docklands. Seafaring is the theme as the Thames reaches Greenwich (▷ 20–21) and then the Thames Barrier.

THE BASICS

🔲 K7
✉ Start point: Westminster Pier, SW1
Ⓦ Westminster
💷 Moderate to expensive
Crown River Cruises
☎ 020 7936 2033, circularcruise.london
City Cruises
☎ 020 7740 0400, citycruises.com
Thames River Services
☎ 020 7930 4097, thamesriverservices.co.uk
Westminster Passenger Service Association
☎ 020 7930 2062, wpsa.co.uk

HIGHLIGHTS

● Medieval Palace
● Raleigh's room
● Imperial State Crown
● Tower ravens
● Grand Punch Bowl, 1829
● St. John's Chapel

TIPS

● It's cheaper to buy tickets online at hrp.org.uk.
● If buying tickets on the day, it's vital to arrive early to avoid lines.

The superbly restored rooms of Edward I's 13th-century palace bring the Tower alive as the royal palace and place of pageantry it was. Don't miss gazing at the Crown Jewels.

Medieval glory The Tower of London is Britain's best medieval fortress. William the Conqueror (1066–87) began it as a show of brute force and Edward I (1272–1307) completed it. William's Caen stone White Tower, built within old Roman walls, was an excellent defence: It was 27m (90ft) high, with walls 4.5m (15ft) thick, and space for soldiers, servants and nobles. Henry III began the inner wall, the moat, his own watergate—and the royal zoo. Edward I built the outer wall, several towers and Traitor's Gate, and moved the Mint and Crown Jewels here.

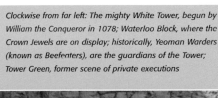

Clockwise from far left: The mighty White Tower, begun by William the Conqueror in 1078; Waterloo Block, where the Crown Jewels are on display; historically, Yeoman Warders (known as Beefeaters), are the guardians of the Tower; Tower Green, former scene of private executions

Wonder and horror Stephen (1135–54) was the first king to live here, James I (1603–25) the last. From here Edward I went in procession to his coronation and Henry VIII paraded through the city bedecked in cloth of gold. The Barons seized the Tower to force King John to put his seal to the Magna Carta in 1215, and two princes were murdered while their uncle was being crowned Richard III. Since 1485 it has been guarded by Yeoman Warders or Beefeaters, who also now give guided tours.

Centuries of history The Tower has been a palace, fortress, state prison and execution site and its gates are still locked every night. If the history is overwhelming there is help in the shape of a welcome area, guided tours, an audio tour and numerous interactive displays.

THE BASICS

hrp.org.uk

⊞ S5

✉ Tower Hill, EC3

☎ 020 3166 6000

🕐 Mar–Oct Tue–Sat 9–5.30, Sun–Mon 10–5.30; Nov–Feb Tue–Sat 9–4.30, Sun–Mon 10–4.30

🍴 Cafés, restaurant

Ⓣ Tower Hill

🚆 Fenchurch Street, London Bridge, Docklands Light Railway (Tower Gateway)

♿ Excellent for Jewel House

✋ Expensive

❓ Free guided tours every 30 min; audio tours

HIGHLIGHTS

● British Galleries
● India and Islamic Galleries
● Jewellery Gallery
● Glass Gallery
● Leonardo da Vinci notebooks
● Silver collection
● Raphael Gallery
● Architecture Gallery
● The Hereford Screen

TIPS

● Explore the new Exhibition Road entrance.
● Join a gallery tour or talk.
● Evening openings have a good atmosphere.

Part of the V&A's glory is that each room is unexpected—it may contain a French boudoir, plaster casts of classical sculptures, antique silver or contemporary glass.

A vision The V&A started as the South Kensington Museum. It was Prince Albert's vision—arts and science objects available to all people to inspire them to invent and create, with the accent on commercial design and craftsmanship. Since it opened in 1857, its collection, now comprising more than a million works, has become so encyclopedic it ranks as the world's largest decorative arts museum.

Bigger and bigger The existing 11km (7 miles) of gallery space over six floors grew even more impressive with the opening in

Clockwise from left: The V&A, which opened in 1857, now ranks as the world's largest museum of decorative arts; exhibits in the museum's The Renaissance City 1350–1600 display; the Jameel Gallery, where exhibits showcase Islamic art from the eighth and ninth centuries

2017 of a grand new entrance hall and ceramic-tiled courtyard on Exhibition Road that includes a state-of-the-art subterranean gallery providing one of the largest temporary exhibition spaces in the UK. The porcelain-tiled courtyard with its glass-fronted café is an exciting venue for installations and events.

Riches and rags Not every object in the museum is precious, and there are everyday things, unique pieces and opportunities to discover a fascination for a new subject—perhaps lace, ironwork, tiles or Japanese textiles. See the lavishly refurbished British and Whiteley Silver galleries, the magnificent collections in the Medieval and Renaissance galleries, the Raphael Cartoons and the striking Ceramics Gallery and Study Centre.

THE BASICS

vam.ac.uk

C8

✉ Cromwell Road, Exhibition Road SW7

☎ 020 7942 2000

🕐 Daily 10–5.45 (Fri until 10)

🍴 Restaurant, cafés

Ⓢ South Kensington

♿ Very good

💰 Free, except some special exhibitions

❓ Free daily guided, introductory tours. Talks, courses, demonstrations, workshops and concerts

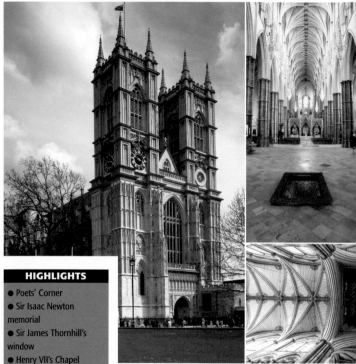

HIGHLIGHTS

● Poets' Corner
● Sir Isaac Newton memorial
● Sir James Thornhill's window
● Henry VII's Chapel
● Edward the Confessor's Chapel
● St. Faith's Chapel
● Grave of the Unknown Soldier
● Little Cloister and College Garden
● Weekday sung evensong at 5pm

TIPS

● Attend a service and hear the choirboys, accompanied by the abbey organ.
● Free organ recitals, Sun 5.45; summer organ festival (mid-Jul to mid-Aug).

The best time to be in the abbey is for the 8am service, sometimes held in St. Faith's Chapel. Follow this with a wander in the nave and cloisters before the crowds arrive.

The kernel of London's second city It was Edward the Confessor who in the 11th century began the rebuilding of the Benedictine abbey church of St. Peter, which was consecrated in 1065. The first sovereign to be crowned there was William the Conqueror in 1066. Successive kings were patrons, as were the pilgrims who flocked to the Confessor's shrine. Henry III (1207–72) employed Master Henry de Reyns to begin the Gothic abbey that stands today, and Henry VII (1457–1509) built his Tudor chapel with its delicate fan vaulting. Since William I, all sovereigns have been crowned

Clockwise from far left: The West Front; the Grave of the Unknown Soldier, adorned with Remembrance Day poppies; the shrine of Edward the Confessor, the abbey's founder; the choir stalls and ornate gilt altar; the abbey's magnificent vaulted ceiling

here—even after Henry VIII broke with Rome in 1533; and all were buried here up to George II (after which Windsor became the royal burial place, ▷ 79). It has also hosted 16 royal marriages, including that of Prince William and Kate Middleton in 2011.

Daunting riches The abbey is massive, full of monuments, and very popular. From the nave's west end enjoy the view of the abbey, then look over the Victorian Gothic choir screen into Henry V's chantry. Having explored the chapels, the royal necropolis and Poets' Corner, leave time for the quiet cloister with superb views of the flying buttresses supporting the nave. The Queen's Diamond Jubilee Galleries, set high up in the medieval triforium and due to open in 2018, will display Abbey treasures.

THE BASICS

westminster-abbey.org

✚ J8

✉ Broad Sanctuary, SW1; entry by North Door

☎ 020 7222 5152

🕐 Abbey: Mon–Sat times vary, call or check website; no photography. Abbey Museum, College Garden: daily various hours. Closed before special services

Ⓜ Westminster, St. James's Park

🚉 Victoria

♿ Good

💷 Expensive

❓ Guided tours, audio guides

More to See

This section contains other great places to visit if you have more time. Some are in the heart of the city while others are a short journey away, found under Farther Afield. This chapter also has fantastic excursions that you should set aside a whole day to visit.

In the Heart of the City 66
30 St. Mary Axe 66
Albert Memorial 66
Apsley House
  (Wellington Museum) 66
Bank of England Museum 66
Borough Market 66
British Library 67
Charles Dickens Museum 67
Churchill War Rooms 67
City Hall 68
Clarence House 68
Cleopatra's Needle 68
Covent Garden Piazza 68
Design Museum 69
Eros 69
Foundling Museum 69
Garden Museum 69
Golden Hinde II 69
Green Park 70
Guildhall Art Gallery 70
Handel & Hendrix in London 70
Hayward Gallery 70
HMS *Belfast* 71
Holy Trinity, Sloane Square 71
Hyde Park 71
Leadenhall Building 71
London Transport Museum 71
Madame Tussauds 72
Peter Pan statue 72
Petrie Museum 72
Photographers' Gallery 72
Regent's Park 73

Royal Academy of Arts 73
St. James's, Piccadilly 73
St. Katharine Docks 73
SEA LIFE London Aquarium 73
The Shard 74
Sir John Soane's Museum 74
Southwark Cathedral 74
Spencer House 74
Temple of Mithras 75
Trafalgar Square 75
Wallace Collection 75
ZSL London Zoo 75

Farther Afield 76
Canary Wharf 76
Chelsea Physic Garden 76
Chiswick House 76
Dulwich Picture Gallery 76
Ham House 76
Hampstead Heath 77
Jewish Museum 77
Kenwood House 77
Kew Gardens 77
London Wetland Centre 77
Museum of London
  Docklands 77
V&A Museum of Childhood 77
Whitechapel Art Gallery 77

Excursions 78
Hampton Court Palace 78
Windsor 79

In the Heart of the City

30 ST. MARY AXE

30stmaryaxe.com

This landmark tower, affectionately known as "The Gherkin," adds wit to the cluster of tall buildings in London's financial hub.

➕ R4 ✉ 30 St. Mary Axe, EC3 🚫 Not open to the general public 🚇 Bank

ALBERT MEMORIAL

royalparks.org.uk

George Gilbert Scott's Gothic extravaganza, dedicated to Prince Albert, celebrates Victorian achievement with marble statues representing the Arts, Sciences, Industry and Continents. The finely carved frieze at its base depicts famous people in the Arts.

➕ B7 ✉ Alexandra Gate, Kensington Gardens, SW7 🚇 South Kensington

APSLEY HOUSE (WELLINGTON MUSEUM)

english-heritage.org.uk

The splendid mansion was built for Arthur Wellesley, Duke of Wellington (1769–1852). The sumptuous interior houses his magnificent collection of paintings and decorative arts, with works by Velázquez and Rubens, as well as silver, porcelain and Canova's nude statue of Napoleon.

➕ F7 ✉ Hyde Park Corner, W1 ☎ 020 7499 5676 🕐 Apr–Oct Wed–Sun 11–5; Nov–Mar Sat–Sun 10–4 🚇 Hyde Park Corner 💷 Moderate

BANK OF ENGLAND MUSEUM

bankofengland.co.uk/education

Exhibits illustrate the history of Britain's monetary and banking system since 1694. Take time to appreciate the re-creations of Soane's rooms and Sir Herbert Baker's Rotunda. The museum stages changing exhibitions.

➕ Q4 ✉ Bartholomew Lane, EC2 ☎ 020 7601 5545 🕐 Mon–Fri 10–5, last admission 4.45 🚇 Bank 💷 Free

BOROUGH MARKET

boroughmarket.org.uk

Top-quality British and international produce is offered at London's oldest and most exciting food market. Many of the traders are artisan producers, keen to share their passion for good food and

The glittering Albert Memorial and nearby Albert Hall

30 St. Mary Axe, dubbed "The Gherkin'"

fine ingredients. Good restaurants and popular cafés complete the attractive scene.

⊞ Q6 ✉ Southwark Street, SE1 🕙 Full market Wed–Thu 10–5, Fri 10–6, Sat 8–5; lunch market Mon–Tue 10–5 🚇 London Bridge 🚉 London Bridge

BRITISH LIBRARY
bl.uk

The library is home to well over 150 million items in most known languages, including maps, manuscripts, prints, drawings, music scores, patents, sound recordings and eight million stamps. Among its many treasures are a 1215 copy of the Magna Carta, original editions of Chaucer's *Canterbury Tales*, the Gutenberg Bible, Shakespeare's first folio, Handel's *Messiah*, Beatles' manuscripts, Leonardo da Vinci's notebook and Captain Scott's diary of his ill-fated Antarctic expedition.

⊞ J1 ✉ 96 Euston Road, NW1 ☎ 0330 333 1144 🕙 Mon–Thu 9.30–8, Fri 9.30–6, Sat 9.30–5, Sun 11–5 🍴 Café, restaurant 🚇 King's Cross, St Pancras 💷 Free; charge for special events and exhibitions

CHARLES DICKENS MUSEUM
dickensmuseum.com

Visit the house where Dickens wrote his novels *Nicholas Nickleby* and *Oliver Twist*. A £3.1 million restoration project has given visitors a real sense of his life and work.

⊞ L2 ✉ 48 Doughty Street, WC1 ☎ 020 7405 2127 🕙 Tue–Sun 10–5, last admission 4 🍴 Café 🚇 Russell Square 💷 Moderate

CHURCHILL WAR ROOMS
iwm.org.uk

Britain's war effort was directed from these secret rooms in a bunker complex beneath Whitehall's streets. The Cabinet War Rooms, where Churchill and his War Cabinet met, offices and dormitories reveal what life was like underground for the hundreds of staff while bombs rained overhead. The Map Room is exactly how it was left when the lights were switched off in August 1945. Interactive displays in the Churchill Museum explore his fascinating life and legacy with

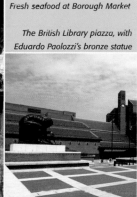

Fresh seafood at Borough Market

The British Library piazza, with Eduardo Paolozzi's bronze statue

personal letters, extracts from speeches, historic documents, photos and film clips.

➕ J7 ✉ Clive Steps, King Charles Street, SW1 ☎ 020 7930 6961 🕐 Daily 9.30–6, last admission 5 🚇 St. James's Park, Westminster 💷 Expensive

CITY HALL

london.gov.uk

Architect Sir Norman Foster's distinctive glass building is the office of the Mayor of London and the capital's governing body, the London Assembly. The Scoop, an outdoor amphitheater, seats 800 for summer events.

➕ R6 ✉ The Queen's Walk, SE1 ☎ 020 7983 4100 🕐 Mon–Thu 8.30–6, Fri 8.30–5.30 🚇 London Bridge 💷 Free

CLARENCE HOUSE

royalcollection.org.uk

Built for Prince William, Duke of Clarence and later William IV, this was the late Queen Mother's London home, now magnificently renovated by its current resident, the Prince of Wales. Five rooms used by Prince Charles and the Duchess of Cornwall for official engagements can be seen. All tickets are timed and must be pre-booked.

➕ H7 ✉ Off the Mall, SW1 ☎ 020 7766 7303 🕐 Guided tours Aug Mon–Fri 10–4.30, Sat–Sun 10–5.30 🚇 St. James's Park, Green Park 💷 Expensive

CLEOPATRA'S NEEDLE

Far older than Cleopatra, this impressive 26m (86ft) pink granite obelisk was constructed in Ancient Egypt in 1450BC and records the triumphs of Rameses the Great.

➕ K6 ✉ Victoria Embankment, WC2 🚇 Embankment, Charing Cross 💷 Free

COVENT GARDEN PIAZZA

coventgarden.london

London's first square was laid out in the 1630s by architect Inigo Jones. It later became a fruit and vegetable market. Redeveloped in the 1980s, the piazza is a popular meeting and eating place, with lively street entertainment.

➕ K5 🍴 Cafés, restaurants and bars 🚇 Covent Garden

City Hall, home to the London Assembly

DESIGN MUSEUM

designmuseum.org

Devoted to contemporary design and architecture, with three galleries under a suitably spectacular roof, the museum tells the story of design and its impact on our lives.

➕ Off map at A7 ✉ 224–238 Kensington High Street, W8 ☎ 020 3862 5900 ⏰ Daily 10–6, last admission 5 🍴 Restaurant, café 🚇 Kensington High Street, Holland Park 💷 Free; temporary exhibitions expensive

EROS

Alfred Gilbert's memorial (1893) to the philanthropic 7th Earl of Shaftesbury (1801–85), *The Angel of Christian Charity*, is popularly referred to as Eros, although it actually depicts Anteros, the god of selfless love.

➕ H5 ✉ Piccadilly Circus, W1 🚇 Piccadilly Circus

FOUNDLING MUSEUM

foundlingmuseum.org.uk

When Thomas Coram founded a hospice for abandoned children in 1739, Handel and Hogarth helped to raise funds. Both the building and the art, which includes paintings by Gainsborough, Hogarth and Millais, are magnificent. The Gerald Coke Handel Collection has amazing material relating to the composer and his contemporaries.

➕ K2 ✉ 40 Brunswick Square, WC1 ☎ 020 7841 3600 ⏰ Tue–Sat 10–5, Sun 11–5 🍴 Café 🚇 Russell Square 💷 Moderate

GARDEN MUSEUM

gardenmuseum.org.uk

Celebrating the plant-hunting Tradescant family and 400 years of garden and plant history in an old church, knot garden and gallery, the Garden Museum was given a £7.5 million transformation in 2017.

➕ L8 ✉ Lambeth Palace Road, SE1 ☎ 020 7401 8865 ⏰ Check website or phone for details 🍴 Café 🚇 Lambeth North 💷 Moderate

GOLDEN HINDE II

goldenhinde.com

The ship is an exact replica of the 16th-century galleon in which

A street performer entertains the crowds at Covent Garden Piazza

Eros, at the heart of Piccadilly Circus

Sir Francis Drake circumnavigated the globe. Take a look at the website for events and tours.

🚼 Q6 ✉ St. Mary Overie Dock, Cathedral Street, SE1 ☎ 020 7403 0123 ⓘ Usually daily 10–5.30, but check online or phone 🍴 Refreshment kiosks 🚇 London Bridge 🚆 London Bridge 💷 Moderate

GREEN PARK

royalparks.org.uk

Covering 19ha (47 acres), Green Park is a popular venue for summer picnics, and famous for its mature trees, tree-lined avenues, grass lawns and attractive spring daffodil displays.

🚼 G7 ✉ SW1 ☎ 0300 061 2350 ⓘ Daily 24 hrs 🚇 Green Park, Hyde Park Corner 💷 Free

GUILDHALL ART GALLERY

cityoflondon.gov.uk

The gallery offers two remarkable things to see: the Guildhall's quirky collection of mostly British pictures, and part of Roman London's huge amphitheater, built in AD200 and rediscovered in 1988. Stop to admire the Guildhall yard too.

🚼 P4 ✉ Guildhall Yard, Gresham Street, EC2 ☎ 020 7332 3700 ⓘ Mon–Sat 10–5, Sun 12–4 🚇 St. Paul's, Bank 💷 Free

HANDEL & HENDRIX IN LONDON

handelhendrix.org

Handel's house is at 25 Brook Street, and Jimi Hendrix's flat is on the top floor of 23. The first was home to the composer of *The Messiah* from 1723 to 1759, while the second was where the American guitarist, singer and songwriter lived for a short time between 1968 and 1969.

🚼 G5 ✉ 25 and 23 Brook Street, W1 ☎ 020 7495 1685 ⓘ Mon–Sat 11–6, last admission 5 🚇 Bond Street, Oxford Circus 💷 Expensive

HAYWARD GALLERY

southbankcentre.co.uk

Housed in a brutalist-style building from the 1960s, the Hayward stages work by pioneering artists. A two-year refurbishment project is restoring 66 glass pyramid roof lights to let natural light into the upper galleries for the first time.

The retired 1938 war cruiser HMS Belfast

➕ L6 ✉ Belvedere Road, SE1 ☎ 020
7960 4200 🕐 Closed; scheduled to reopen
mid-2018 🚇 Waterloo 🚉 Waterloo
💷 Expensive; some exhibitions free

HMS *BELFAST*

iwm.org.uk
Clamber up, down and around
this 1938 war cruiser, visiting the
cabins, gun turrets, dining hall,
bridge and boiler room to get a
taste of life on board a warship.
Real-life accounts of some of the
950-strong crew help to bring it
all to life.
➕ R6 ✉ The Queen's Walk, SE1 ☎ 020
7940 6300 🕐 Apr–Oct daily 10–6; Nov–
Feb daily 10–5 🍴 Café 🚇 London Bridge
🚉 London Bridge 💷 Expensive

HOLY TRINITY, SLOANE SQUARE

holytrinitysloanesquare.co.uk
London's best Arts and Crafts
church, designed by J.D. Sedding,
has glass by Burne-Jones, William
Morris and others. Note the huge
east window with its 48 panels
depicting saints.
➕ E9 ✉ Sloane Square, SW1 ☎ 020
7730 7270 🕐 Daily 9–5 🚇 Sloane Square
💷 Donation

HYDE PARK

royalparks.org.uk
One of city's largest open spaces,
the park was tamed in the 18th
century and is the perfect place for
a picnic. Don't miss the views from
the Serpentine Bridge, the Rose
Garden or the Diana, Princess of
Wales Memorial Fountain.
➕ E6 ✉ W2 ☎ 0300 061 2114 🕐 Daily
5am–midnight 🍴 Restaurant, café
🚇 Knightsbridge, Lancaster Gate, Hyde Park
Corner 💷 Free

LEADENHALL BUILDING

theleadenhallbuilding.com
The 224m (734ft) "Cheesegrater,"
London's newest skyscraper
opened in 2015 in the heart of
the financial district. The stunning
glass and steel construction was
designed by Richard Rogers.
➕ R4 ✉ 122 Leadenhall Street, EC3
🕐 Limited public access 🚇 Bank

LONDON TRANSPORT MUSEUM

ltmuseum.co.uk
With beautifully restored old
buses, trams, trolleybuses and
underground rail vehicles, themed
galleries tell the story of London's

The Diana, Princess of Wales Memorial Fountain, Hyde Park

transport system and 200 years of social history.

🔢 K5 ✉ Covent Garden Piazza, WC2
☎ 020 7379 6344 🕐 Sat–Thu 10–6, Fri 11–6, last admission 5.15 🍴 Café
Ⓜ Covent Garden 🚆 Charing Cross
💷 Expensive; free for under 17s

MADAME TUSSAUDS

madametussauds.com/London

See how many famous people you can identify, from Shakespeare to Prince Harry and Donald Trump, or try your hand at being a judge on singing talent contest show *The Voice* alongside will.i.am.

🔢 E3 ✉ Marylebone Road, NW1 ☎ 0333 321 2001 🕐 Hours vary, check website for details 🍴 Café Ⓜ Baker Street
💷 Expensive; family ticket

PETER PAN STATUE

George Frampton's bronze statue (1912) commemorating J.M. Barrie's fictional creation, Peter Pan, the boy who never grew up, stands in Kensington Gardens, west of the Long Water.

🔢 B6 ✉ Long Water, Kensington Gardens, W2 Ⓜ Lancaster Gate

PETRIE MUSEUM

ucl.ac.uk/museums/petrie

The ancient spoils of many Egyptologists' explorations are on display at the hard-to-find Petrie Museum (it's close to the rear of the British Museum). With 80,000 objects, it's one of the world's greatest collections of Egyptian and Sudanese archaeology.

🔢 J2 ✉ University College London, Malet Place, WC1 ☎ 020 7679 2884 🕐 Tue–Sat 1–5 Ⓜ Euston Square 💷 Free

PHOTOGRAPHERS' GALLERY

thephotographersgallery.org.uk

An Edwardian warehouse has been transformed into a state-of-the-art home for the Photographers' Gallery. The gallery has three floors of exhibition space, a bookshop and café, and hosts a range of talks and events, including a prestigious annual photography competition.

🔢 H4 ✉ 16–18 Ramillies Street, W1 ☎ 020 7087 9300 🕐 Mon–Sat 10–6, Thu until 8 during exhibitions, Sun 11–6
Ⓜ Oxford Circus 💷 Inexpensive; free Mon–Fri 10–12 and for under 16s

The London Transport Museum celebrates the capital's transport system

Wax figures at Madame Tussauds

REGENT'S PARK

royalparks.org.uk; zsl.org

Enjoy the vast rose gardens, boating lake, sports facilities and the open-air theater in the summer.
🚇 D1–F2 ✉ Regent's Park, NW1 ☎ 0300 061 2300 🕐 Daily from 5am. Closing times change seasonally 🍽 Cafés Ⓜ Regent's Park, Camden Town 💷 Free

ROYAL ACADEMY OF ARTS

royalacademy.org.uk

The Royal Academy hosts major art shows, plus the annual Summer Exhibition, held every year since 1769. Don't miss the rooftop Sackler Galleries. A major redevelopment is opening up new areas to celebrate the RA's 250th anniversary in 2018.
🚇 H5 ✉ Burlington House, Piccadilly, W1 ☎ 020 7300 8090 🕐 Daily 10–6, Fri until 10 🍽 Restaurant, café Ⓜ Green Park, Piccadilly Circus 💷 Expensive

ST. JAMES'S, PICCADILLY

sjp.org.uk

Wren's church (1682–84), built for the local aristocracy, has a sumptuous interior. Some superb concerts are held here and the courtyard hosts market stalls.
🚇 H6 ✉ 197 Piccadilly, W1 ☎ 020 7734 4511 🕐 Check website or phone for times 🍽 Café Ⓜ Piccadilly Circus 💷 Donation

ST. KATHARINE DOCKS

skdocks.co.uk

Luxury yachts now fill the marina close to Tower Bridge where cargoes were once landed, while restaurants, shops and apartments fill the former warehouses. Explore the World Food Market at Marble Quay on Friday lunchtimes 11–3.
🚇 S6 ✉ St. Katharine's Way, E1 ☎ 020 7264 5287 Ⓜ Tower Hill 🚈 Tower Gateway (DLR), Fenchurch Street 🚢 Tower Pier, St. Katharine's Pier 💷 Free

SEA LIFE LONDON AQUARIUM

visitsealife.com/london

More than 3,000 forms of marine life, including sharks, stingrays and turtles, fill this aquatic spectacular. Stroke a crab in the rock pool exhibit or catch a piranha feeding frenzy in the rainforest section.
🚇 L7 ✉ County Hall, SE1 🕐 Daily 10–7 Ⓜ Westminster, Waterloo 💷 Expensive

The Royal Academy of Arts

St. Katharine Docks

THE SHARD

theviewfromtheshard.com

Occupying floors 68–72 of The Shard, London's tallest landmark at 310m (1,016ft), The View offers uninterrupted 360-degree panoramas across the city and beyond.

➕ Q6 ✉ Joiner Street, SE1
☎ 0344 499 7111 ⏱ Apr–Oct daily 10–10; Nov–Mar Sun–Wed 10–7, Thu–Sat 10–10. Last admission 1 hour before closing. Timed tickets, pre-booking advised
🚇 London Bridge 🚉 London Bridge
🎟 Expensive

SIR JOHN SOANE'S MUSEUM

soane.org

The gloriously overfurnished home of neoclassical architect and avid collector Sir John Soane (1753–1837) is full of surprises. Canaletto's paintings hang in the breakfast room, Hogarth's *Rake's Progress* unfolds from the walls, and there's even an Egyptian pharaoh's sarcophagus downstairs. There are so many sculptures, paintings and antiquities packing every surface that unless you keep your eyes peeled you are likely to miss a Watteau drawing or a rare Etruscan vase.

➕ L4 ✉ 13 Lincoln's Inn Fields, WC2
☎ 020 7405 2107 ⏱ Tue–Sat 10–5, last admission 4.30 🚉 London Bridge
🚇 Holborn 🎟 Free, donation

SOUTHWARK CATHEDRAL

cathedral.southwark.anglican.org

The imposing stone building is powerfully atmospheric of its medieval origins, despite much rebuilding over the centuries. Inside, there are fine choir stalls and some interesting monuments.

➕ Q6 ✉ London Bridge, SE1
☎ 020 7367 6700 ⏱ Mon–Fri 8–6, Sat–Sun 8.30–6 🍴 Café 🚇 London Bridge 🚉 London Bridge 🎟 Donation

SPENCER HOUSE

spencerhouse.co.uk

A lavishly restored Palladian mansion, Spencer House is a rare survivor of 18th-century aristocratic St. James's and Mayfair. Eight rooms with gilded decorations, period paintings and furniture are open to the public, along with the authentically restored garden.

Southwark Cathedral retains a medieval appearance despite much rebuilding

The Picture Room in Sir John Soane's Museum

H6 27 St. James's Place, SW1 020 7514 1958 Sun from 10.30 (last tour 4.30). Closed Aug. Guided tours only Green Park Expensive; no children under 10

TEMPLE OF MITHRAS
The Roman temple foundations of AD240–50 testify to the cult of the Persian god Mithras.
P5 Temple Court, Queen Victoria Street, EC4 Mansion House, Bank

TRAFALGAR SQUARE
Sir Edwin Landseer's lions protect Nelson's Column, erected to commemorate the 1805 Battle of Trafalgar, at the heart of this iconic square. The fountains were added in 1845. Bronze statues occupy three of the plinths; the fourth hosts changing works by contemporary artists.
J6 Restaurants and cafés Charing Cross Charing Cross Free

WALLACE COLLECTION
wallacecollection.org
Works by Velázquez, Titian, Rubens and Rembrandt and exquisite French furniture, Sèvres porcelain and a spectacular array of princely arms and armor are elegantly displayed in a historic London town house, with a notable restaurant in the glass-roofed courtyard.
F4 Hertford House, Manchester Square, W1 020 7563 9500 Daily 10–5 Restaurant, café Marble Arch, Bond Street Free

ZSL LONDON ZOO
zsl.org
More than 750 species call London Zoo home and, from the penguin beach to the new £5.7m, Indian-themed Land of the Lions, their accommodations can be impressive. With walk-through enclosures to meet monkeys and lemurs, environments as diverse as rainforest and tiger territory, daily demonstrations, talks and feeds, the zoo is very popular for a family day out.
Off map at G1 Outer Circle, Regents Park, NW1 020 7722 3333 Daily from 10; closing times vary Restaurants, cafés Regents Park, Camden Town Expensive

Bustling Trafalgar Square, a popular meeting place

Farther Afield

CANARY WHARF

canarywharf.com

Scintillating modern architecture dominates this premier business, shopping and leisure district that has arisen like another city on former docklands.

➕ See map ➤ 115 ✉ Canary Wharf, E14 ☎ 020 7477 1477 ◷ Mon–Fri 9–8, Sat 10–7, Sun 12–6. Individual shops, bars and restaurants may differ ◉ Canary Wharf

CHELSEA PHYSIC GARDEN

chelseaphysicgarden.co.uk

One of London's hidden gems, this walled garden was founded in 1673 to train apothecaries' apprentices in the identification of medicinal plants. Today it is a peaceful oasis by the Thames.

➕ See map ➤ 114 ✉ 66 Royal Hospital Road, SW3 ☎ 020 7352 5646 ◷ Apr–Oct Tue–Fri, Sun 11–6; Nov–Mar Mon–Fri 10–dusk ꠸ Café (Apr–Oct only) ◉ Sloane Square ✋ Expensive

CHISWICK HOUSE

chgt.org.uk

Lord Burlington's exquisite country villa (1725–29), inspired by the architecture of ancient Rome, has superb formal gardens and conservatories.

➕ See map ➤ 114 ✉ Burlington Lane, W4 ☎ 020 8995 0508 ◷ House: Apr–Oct Sun–Wed 10–5. Garden: daily 7–dusk ꠸ Café ◉ Turnham Green ꠨ Chiswick ✋ House: moderate. Garden: free

DULWICH PICTURE GALLERY

dulwichpicturegallery.org.uk

Opened in 1814 as England's first purpose-built, public art gallery, it is home to one of the world's finest collections of Old Master paintings.

➕ See map ➤ 115 ✉ Gallery Road, SE21 ☎ 020 8693 5254 ◷ Tue–Sun 10–5 ꠸ Café ꠨ North or West Dulwich ✋ Moderate

HAM HOUSE

nationaltrust.org.uk

Immerse yourself in the 17th century in this courtier's stately home that's packed with exotic treasures, and explore the kitchen gardens.

➕ See map ➤ 114 ✉ Ham, Richmond, Surrey, TW10 ☎ 020 8940 1950 ◷ Check website or phone for details ꠸ Café ◉ Richmond, then bus 371 ✋ Expensive

Historic Ham House and gardens, built in 1610 on the banks of the Thames

The Museum of London Docklands

HAMPSTEAD HEATH

cityoflondon.gov.uk

Hampstead Heath offers 325ha (800 acres) of open countryside to enjoy in north London.

➕ See map ▷ 114 ✉ Hampstead, NW3 ☎ 020 7482 7073 for visitor information 🚇 Hampstead 💷 Free

JEWISH MUSEUM

jewishmuseum.org.uk

This vibrant Camden Town museum explores the history of Jewish people in Britain.

➕ See map ▷ 114 ✉ 129–131 Albert Street, NW1 ☎ 020 7284 7384 🕐 Sat–Thu 10–5, Fri 10–2 🍴 Kosher café 🚇 Camden Town 💷 Moderate

KENWOOD HOUSE

english-heritage.org.uk

Restyled by Robert Adam, this country house lies outside pretty Hampstead village in north London. Its walls are hung with Rembrandts, Romneys, Vermeers and Gainsboroughs and its landscaped parkland provides grand views. In summer, evening concerts are held in the grounds.

➕ See map ▷ 114 ✉ Hampstead Lane, NW3 ☎ 020 8348 1286 🕐 Daily 10–5 🍴 Café 🚇 Hampstead Heath 💷 Free

KEW GARDENS

kew.org

With 44,000 plants and some glorious glasshouses, the 120ha (300-acre) Royal Botanic Garden at Kew is a magical place. Walks on tree-shaded avenues, mesmerizing flower displays, a treetop walkway, a unique multi-sensory giant beehive and the restored Kew Palace are just some of the attractions.

➕ See map ▷ 114 ✉ Richmond, Surrey, TW9 ☎ 020 8332 5655 🕐 Daily from 10; see website for closing times 🍴 Café 🚇 Kew Gardens 🚉 Richmond, then bus 65 💷 Expensive

LONDON WETLAND CENTRE

wwt.org.uk

The Wildfowl and Wetlands Trust administers 42ha (104 acres) of lakes, ponds, grassland and mud-flats that attract a variety of wildlife.

➕ See map ▷ 114 ✉ Queen Elizabeth's Walk, SW13 ☎ 020 8409 4400 🕐 Mar–Oct daily 9.30–5.30; Nov–Feb 9.30–4.30; last admission 1 hour before closing 🍴 Café 🚇 Hammersmith, then bus 33, 72, 209 🚉 Barnes, then bus 33, 72 💷 Expensive

MUSEUM OF LONDON DOCKLANDS

museumoflondon.org.uk/docklands

The museum tells the story of London's river, port and people from Roman times until now.

➕ See map ▷ 115 ✉ No. 1 Warehouse, West India Quay, E14 ☎ 020 7001 9844 🕐 Daily 10–6 🍴 Restaurant, café 🚇 West India Quay, Canary Wharf 💷 Free

V&A MUSEUM OF CHILDHOOD

vam.ac.uk/moc

Exhibits here explore playtime from 1600 to the present day, with Noah's arks, dolls, toy soldiers, games and mechanical toys.

➕ See map ▷ 115 ✉ Cambridge Heath Road, E2 ☎ 020 8983 5200 🕐 Daily 10–5.45 🍴 Café 🚇 Bethnal Green 🚉 Bethnal Green 💷 Free

WHITECHAPEL ART GALLERY

whitechapelgallery.org

This is the influential hub of East End contemporary art (▷ 6–7).

➕ S4 ✉ 77–82 Whitechapel High Street, E1 ☎ 020 7522 7888 🕐 Tue–Wed, Fri–Sun 11–6, Thu 11–9 🍴 Café 🚇 Aldgate East 💷 Free

Excursions

HAMPTON COURT PALACE

hrp.org.uk

This is London's most impressive royal palace, well worth the 35-minute train journey from central London.

When King Henry VIII dismissed Cardinal Wolsey in 1529, he took over his already ostentatious Tudor palace and enlarged it. Successive monarchs altered and repaired both the palace and its 12ha (29 acres) of beautiful Tudor and baroque gardens.

The best way to visit this huge collection of chambers, courtyards and state apartments is to follow one of the six clearly indicated routes—perhaps Henry VIII's State Apartments or the King's Apartments built for William III, immaculately restored after a devastating fire. Highlights include Henry VIII's Great Hall, which is recognized as England's finest medieval hall. William Shakespeare performed plays here between 1603 and 1604. The Chapel Royal, still in use after 450 years, should not be missed. Neither should the vast Tudor kitchens, built to feed Henry VIII's court, providing more than 600 meals twice a day. Live cookery demonstrations are given every month; check the website for dates of these and other events.

You can easily spend a day at the palace, but allow at least three hours for your visit. Do not miss the formal Tudor gardens that reach down to the River Thames, the famous Maze and restored Privy Garden, looking now as it would have done when it was created for William III in 1702.

Children love Hampton Court, not least because there are so many events and activities designed especially for them, including costumed presentations and family audio guides and trails.

Distance: 22.5km (14 miles)
Journey time: 35 min
✉ East Molesey, Surrey, KT8
🕐 Apr–Oct daily 10–6; Nov–Mar 10–4.30
🍴 Café, restaurant 🚉 Waterloo to Hampton Court 🚢 Riverboat to Hampton Court 💷 Expensive

The beautiful formal flower gardens at Hampton Court Palace

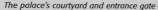

The palace's courtyard and entrance gate

WINDSOR

windsor.gov.uk;
royalcollection.org.uk

Fairy-tale towers and turrets make this the ultimate royal castle. An official residence of Her Majesty the Queen, it's the oldest and largest occupied castle in the world. As it is a working royal palace, opening times can change, so check the website for the latest information. A typical tour lasts between two and three hours.

Begun by William the Conqueror and rebuilt in stone by Henry II, the castle has been embellished over the centuries. The richly deco-rated State Apartments are hung with paintings by Old Masters, including Rembrandt, Rubens and Canaletto. The tombs of 10 sover-eigns, including Henry VIII and Charles I, lie amid the fine Gothic architecture of St. George's Chapel, setting for the service of dedication following the marriage of Prince Charles and the Duchess of Cornwall in 2005.

Should the State Apartments or Chapel be closed, there is still much to see. The Drawings Gallery has changing exhibitions, and don't miss Queen Mary's Dolls' House, designed by Edward Lutyens. Some 1,500 craftspeople were involved in its construction.

Changing the Guard takes place at 11am daily from April to the end of July, and on alternate days for the rest of the year, weather permitting, but never on Sundays.

Outside the castle lie Windsor's medieval cobblestoned lanes, Christopher Wren's Guildhall and the Theatre Royal. Beyond it, you can explore 1,950ha (4,820-acre) Windsor Great Park and cross the river footbridge to Eton.

Distance: 40km (25 miles)
Journey time: 40–55 min
Windsor Tourist Information
✉ Windsor Royal Shopping, Thames Street, SL4 ☎ 01753 743900 ◷ Check website for opening times 🚉 Waterloo to Windsor & Eton Riverside, Paddington to Windsor & Eton Central
Windsor Castle
◷ Check website for opening times
💷 Expensive

Stately Windsor Castle

Great Park and the Long Walk entrance to Windsor Castle

City Tours

This section contains self-guided tours that will help you explore the sights in each of the city's regions. Each tour is designed to take a day, with a map pinpointing the recommended places along the way. There is a quick reference guide at the end of each tour, listing everything you need in that region, so you know exactly what's close by.

South Bank	82
Fleet Street to the Tower	88
Covent Garden to Regent's Park	94
Westminster and St. James's	100
Around Hyde Park	106
Farther Afield	112

CITY TOURS

South Bank

With sweeping river views, exciting contemporary art at Tate Modern, medieval history at Southwark Cathedral, world-class concert halls and a theatrical tradition dating back to Shakespeare's time, the South Bank has plenty to entice visitors.

Morning
Start at **Tower Bridge** and set the scene for your day with high-level, panoramic views, spotting London's tallest landmark, **The Shard** (▷ 74). Then stroll among the converted warehouses of Shad Thames, home to numerous shops and cafés. Join the well-signed riverside Thames Path, passing the distinctive **City Hall** (▷ 68), seat of London's government, and the moored war cruiser **HMS** *Belfast* (right, ▷ 71).

Mid-morning
From Tooley Street, zigzag under **London Bridge** to visit **Southwark Cathedral** (left, ▷ 74). Admire the soaring nave, choir and 16th-century Great Screen, and look for stained-glass windows depicting famous Southwark inhabitants, including Chaucer and Shakespeare. The **Harvard Chapel** reveals some of the cathedral's many links with America.

Lunch
Borough Market (right, ▷ 66–67) is nearby and the perfect location for lunch, especially Wednesdays to Saturdays when it's packed with enticing food stalls and the restaurants are particularly lively.

Afternoon

Return to the riverside, passing the fine
14th-century rose window in the ruins of
Winchester Palace, to see the replica of
Sir Francis Drake's magnificent galleon,
Golden Hinde II (right, ▷ 69–70). Walk
through medieval Clink Street, once the
site of a notorious prison. Passing under
Southwark Bridge, restaurants, cafés and
pubs with river views line the route to
Shakespeare's Globe (▷ 48–49), a
faithful reconstruction of an Elizabethan
open-air theater. The excellent guided
tour of the theater is not to be missed.

Mid-afternoon

Explore the contemporary art at **Tate Modern**
(▷ 54–55) and take time for tea in its café with a
view. Continue your stroll along the Thames Path,
enjoying views of the architecture lining the opposite
bank of the river. Have a look in the crafts studios on
the lower floors of the **Oxo Tower** (left) and in
nearby **Gabriel's Wharf**, before you reach **Waterloo
Bridge**—you may find a secondhand books market
under its arches—and the **Southbank Centre**.

Dinner

There's a vast choice of restaurants around here, but if you're up for
somewhere smart with unmatched views, book a table at the **Oxo
Tower Bar, Brasserie and Restaurant** (▷ 149).

Evening

With concerts by world-class musicians at
the **Royal Festival Hall** (▷ 138), plays
at the **National Theatre** (▷ 136) and
films at **BFI Southbank** (▷ 133), you're
spoiled for choice for entertainment in
this part of London. Free live music events
are often held in the early evening. A ride
on the **London Eye** (▷ 30–31) at night
is a magical experience.

Lincoln's Inn Fields
Royal College of Surgeons & Hunterian Museum
Old Curiosity Shop
St Clement's Lane
London School of Economics & Political Science
Royal Courts of Justice
Inns of Court
Temple Church
Inner Temple
Middle Temple

Bream's Buildings
Maughan Library King's College London
Dr Johnson's House
St Bride's Church
LUDGATE CIRCUS
Old Bailey (Central Criminal Court)
Paternoster Square
London Stock Exchange

CITY THAMESLINK STATION
CITY THAMESLINK STATION
Carter Lane
Castle

KINGSWAY
CHANCERY LANE
FETTER LANE
FLEET STREET
Fleet Street
Ludgate Hill
Queen Victoria
Queen Victoria Street

BLACKFRIARS STATION
PUDDLE DOCK
BLACKFRIARS BRIDGE
Blackfriars
Blackfriars Pier

4

London Transport Museum
St Mary le Strand
India House
Australia House
St Clement Danes
Roman Bath
Courtauld Gallery
King's College

STRAND
ALDWYCH
A4
Temple Place
VICTORIA EMBANKMENT

5 Somerset House
Gilbert Collection

HQS Wellington (Master Mariners)
HMS President
Blackfriars Millennium Pier
BLACKFRIARS BRIDGE
Bankside Gallery
Purdy Hicks Gallery

T h a m e s

6
Cleopatra's Needle
Embankment Pier
Victoria Embankment Gardens
Savoy Pier
Savoy Place
WATERLOO BRIDGE
Festival Pier
Queen Elizabeth Hall
Southbank Centre
BFI Southbank
National Theatre
The London Television Centre
Oxo Tower
Gabriel's Wharf
Upper Ground
STAMFORD STREET
London Nautical School
A3200
SOUTHWARK
GOLDEN JUBILEE BRIDGES
HUNGERFORD BRIDGE
Royal Festival Hall
Hayward Gallery
Schiller University
King's College London
BFI London IMAX Cinema
Shell Centre
Jubilee Gardens
BLACKFRIARS
WATERLOO ROAD

7
London Eye
Waterloo Millennium Pier
London Dungeon
County Hall
SEA LIFE London Aquarium
WESTMINSTER BRIDGE ROAD
A23
WATERLOO STATION
WATERLOO EAST STATION
Southwark College
UNION STREET
THE CUT
Nelson Square
Copperfield
Loman Street
WATERLOO ROAD
Webber Street

Florence Nightingale Museum
St Thomas' Hospital
LAMBETH PALACE ROAD
WESTMINSTER BRIDGE
LAMBETH NORTH
BAYLIS ROAD
KENNINGTON ROAD
ST GEORGE'S CIRCUS
BOROUGH
BOROUGH ROAD
South Bank University

8
LAMBETH
Archbishop's Park
Lambeth Palace
Garden Museum
A3203
Imperial War Museum
Geraldine Mary Harmsworth Park
St George's Cathedral
ST GEORGE'S ROAD
LONDON ROAD
Elephant & Castle
London College of Communication
NEWINGTON

9
Thames Path
Old Paradise Street
500 m
500 yds
Metropolitan Tabernacle
Elephant & Castle Leisure Centre
NEWINGTON BUTTS
KENNINGTON PARK ROAD
A3204
KENNINGTON ROAD

L VAUXHALL   **M**   **N**

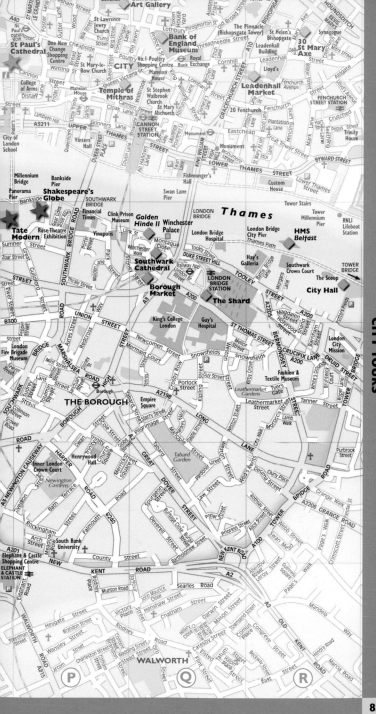

TOP 25 SIGHTS AND EXPERIENCES

Imperial War Museum (▷ 24)
The First World War galleries are a highlight in this museum, focusing on the social impact of warfare through film, painting and sound archives. The atrium has been redesigned by Foster + Partners and displays a number of large exhibits.

London Eye (▷ 30)
On a clear day you can see 40km (25 miles) from the top, across London and as far as Windsor Castle (▷ 79). With four million people stepping on board every year to enjoy the bird's-eye views, it is Britain's most popular paid tourist attraction.

Shakespeare's Globe (▷ 48)
Shakespeare's Globe was built as a result of the passionate vision of Sam Wanamaker. As well as a faithful reconstruction of the Bard's open-air theater, the site also includes a smaller, candlelit theater named for the American actor who created this impressive South Bank landmark.

Tate Modern (▷ 54)
At the foot of the Millennium Bridge and presenting a distinctive face to the Thames, Tate Modern welcomes nearly five million visitors each year. The building itself, a converted power station, is almost as fascinating as the art.

MORE TO SEE 64

Borough Market
City Hall
Garden Museum
Golden Hinde II
Hayward Gallery
HMS *Belfast*
SEA LIFE London Aquarium

The Shard
Southwark Cathedral

ENTERTAINMENT 128

Clubs
Ministry of Sound
Film
BFI IMAX
BFI Southbank
Opera, Ballet and Concerts
Purcell Room
Queen Elizabeth Hall
Royal Festival Hall

Theaters
National Theatre
Old Vic
Shakespeare's Globe
Young Vic

EAT 140

British and Modern
Oxo Tower Bar, Brasserie
   and Restaurant
Roast
European
Baltic

Gastropubs/Bars
Anchor Bankside
Anchor & Hope
Lighter Bites
Tate Modern Café

Waterloo Bridge and Thames Path

Fleet Street to the Tower

On this tour, see where the Romans founded Londinium in the first century AD and discover the city's long and fascinating history through its architecture, from Sir Christopher Wren's magnificent churches to the great Tower of London, with stories to capture everyone's imagination.

Morning
Arrive early at **St. Paul's Cathedral** (right, ▷ 44–45) before the crowds descend to appreciate fully its magnificence. The cathedral opens for sightseeing at 8.30am, but there are services, usually at 7.30am and 8am, which you could attend. Pâtisserie **Paul** (▷ 126) in Paternoster Square is the perfect place to stop for a snack.

Mid-morning
Walk up St. Martin's Aldersgate to the **Museum of London** (left, ▷ 32–33) and spend some time exploring its excellent collection. Retracing your steps, turn left into Gresham Street. Ahead is **St. Lawrence Jewry** church, with dark wooden pews and a gold-encrusted ceiling lit by chandeliers. Cross the Guildhall Square to visit the **Guildhall Art Gallery** (▷ 70).

Lunch
Walk down King Street and turn right into Cheapside for an early lunch at **The Café Below** (▷ 145) in the crypt of **St. Mary-le-Bow**, a Wren church with striking modern stained-glass windows. A statue of Captain John Smith (1580–1631), leader of the Virginia Colony at Jamestown, presides over the square.

Afternoon

After lunch, turn down Bow Churchyard passage, then turn right into Bow Lane, lined with smart shops and eateries, to cross Watling Street. On the left is the **Guild Church of St. Mary Aldermary**. It's worth stepping inside to admire the magnificent ceiling.

The ruins of the **Temple of Mithras** (▷ 75) stand amid the soaring glass-and-steel modernity of the City's financial institutions. Ahead you'll see the distinctive **30 St. Mary Axe** (▷ 66), known as "The Gherkin." Passing the great pillars of the **Mansion House**, with the Bank of England in view, do some window-shopping in the **Royal Exchange** (right, ▷ 126) before exploring the food stands in **Leadenhall Market** (▷ 125–126).

Mid-afternoon

Head down Philpot Lane to the Thames, pausing to admire Wren's towering **Monument** (to the Great Fire of London) on your right. The riverside Customs House Walkway will lead you to the **Tower of London** (below, ▷ 58–59). Aim to arrive by 2pm. Ideally you will have prebooked your entrance ticket to avoid any waiting around. First, take a tour with one of the Yeoman Warders, then spend the rest of the afternoon soaking up the history.

Evening

Sit by the Thames and enjoy the views of Tower Bridge and the south bank of the river. Walk through to **St. Katharine Docks** (▷ 73) and stroll among the smart yachts in the marina. The renovated warehouses there house a host of bars and restaurants in which to relax. Alternatively, take the Circle Line from Tower Hill to Farringdon for a gastropub experience at **The Peasant** (▷ 149).

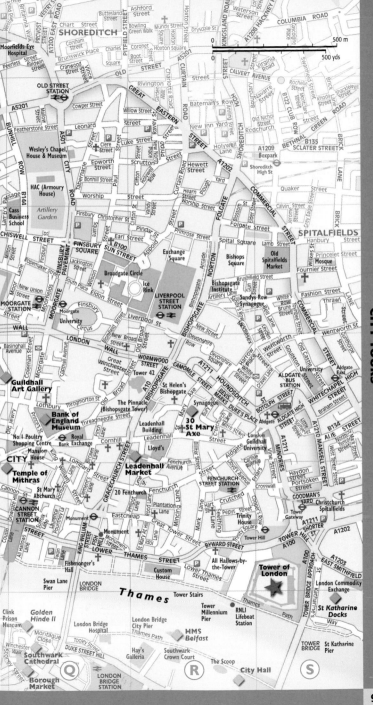

Fleet Street to the Tower
Quick Reference Guide

CITY TOURS

Museum of London (▷ 32)
There is no better place to get an overview of the city's history, from prehistoric times to the present day, than at this museum. Its fascinating exhibits are so well displayed, it would be hard not to be engrossed. The museum even stands where the city first began, on the site of the Roman fort.

St. Paul's Cathedral (▷ 44)
Five monarchs oversaw the building of Sir Christopher Wren's masterpiece, completed in 1710, and ever since it has been the place where events of national importance are celebrated, mourned and commemorated. Come in the early evening, to listen to the choir sing evensong.

Tower of London (▷ 58)
As it is one of London's most popular sights, it's definitely worth prebooking your entry tickets for the Tower, especially during the high-season summer months. A tour with a Yeoman Warder (known as a Beefeater) as your guide is an experience that you'll always remember.

MORE TO SEE   64

30 St. Mary Axe
Bank of England Museum
Guildhall Art Gallery

Leadenhall Building
St. Katharine Docks
Temple of Mithras

SHOP · 118

Fashion
The Goodhood Store
Luna & Curious

Shopping Centers
Royal Exchange
Street Markets
Leadenhall Market

ENTERTAINMENT · 128

Clubs
Fabric
Opera, Ballet and Concerts
Barbican Centre

Theaters
Barbican Centre

EAT · 140

Asian
Banh Mi Bay
British and Modern
The Café Below
St. John
European
Club Gascon

Famous Chefs
Fifteen
Gastropubs/Bars
The Peasant
Lighter Bites
Wren's Pantry
Vegetarian
Vanilla Black

CITY TOURS

St. Paul's and the Millennium Bridge

Covent Garden to Regent's Park

Literary associations, museums great and quirky, fine art and fun shopping all combine on this walk, which takes in busy streets and quiet corners. Here you'll find Theatreland, the heart of London's entertainment industry, lively Chinatown and Soho.

Morning

From Holborn Underground station, turn off Kingsway to enter Lincoln's Inn Fields. On its northern side, **Sir John Soane's Museum** (left, ▷ 74) is wonderfully atmospheric. As you cross the leafy square, look to the left to see the impressive brick buildings of Lincoln's Inn, one of the Inns of Court. With its outdoor terraces and open kitchen, **Fields Bar & Kitchen**, at the heart of Lincoln's Inn Fields, may tempt you to a coffee or something more substantial, before continuing on to **The Old Curiosity Shop**, built in 1567, immortalized by Charles Dickens and now displaying handmade shoes. Following St. Clement's Lane will take you through the London School of Economics' campus and out alongside the Royal Courts of Justice to the Strand, where Wren's **St. Clement Danes Church** sits on an island amid busy traffic.

Mid-morning

Continue west along the Strand to **Somerset House** (▷ 50–51) to admire the great courtyard and immerse yourself in French Impressionist art at the **Courtauld Gallery** (below, ▷ 51).

Lunch

Eat lunch in grand surroundings in Somerset House or walk up Wellington Street into lively **Covent Garden**, which is packed with cafés, restaurants and bars. **Joe Allen** (▷ 147) is a favorite. Turn left for the **Piazza** (▷ 68). Here you can shop and enjoy the buzz in the former market (right). Cross Long Acre for the trendy shops on Neal Street.

Afternoon

Passing the brightly colored high-rise blocks on St. Giles High Street, visit **St. Giles-in-the-Fields**, a handsome church with a Palladian interior, founded by Queen Matilda in 1101 as a leper hospital. Continue down Denmark Street, famed for its music connections, and cross Charing Cross Road with Foyles, London's most famous bookshop, on the left, to reach leafy **Soho Square**. In the 17th century, this was one of the most fashionable places to live. Today the area is home to the film and recording industries and numerous pubs and restaurants.

Mid-afternoon

Leave at Frith Street, go right at **The Dog and Duck** pub (▷ 146), and stop for refreshment as you zigzag your way through cobbled Meard Street and across Wardour Street to the lively fruit and textiles **market** on Berwick Street. A left turn on Broadwick Street and another left down Lexington Street will take you to the specialist shops of Brewer Street and back onto Wardour Street. Cross Shaftesbury Avenue and turn left into Gerrard Street, the start of **Chinatown**.

Evening

Stroll through **Chinatown** (right) and pick a restaurant that takes your fancy. Shaftesbury Avenue is the heart of **Theatreland**, **Piccadilly Circus** is a short walk away and **Soho** buzzes with restaurants and nightlife.

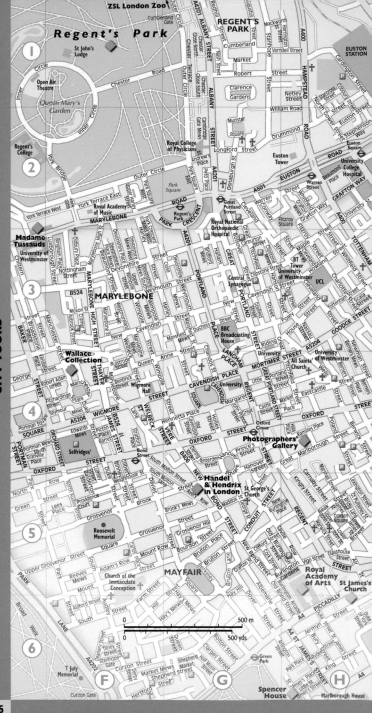

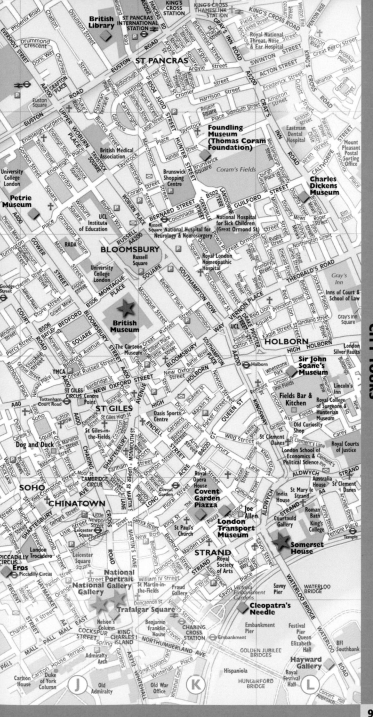

Covent Garden to Regent's Park
Quick Reference Guide

British Museum (▷ 16)

This is one of the world's greatest museums, where you can travel the globe through exhibits from every civilization, spanning some two million years of human history. World-famous objects include the Rosetta Stone, Parthenon sculptures and Egyptian mummies. With eight million artifacts in the collection, excellent special exhibitions, events, talks and activities, you may find you visit more than once.

Somerset House (▷ 50)

In summer, fountains play in the courtyard; in winter it becomes an outdoor ice rink. Whenever you visit, there's likely to be something happening, from contemporary art and design exhibitions to open-air concerts and films. Twice a year it hosts London Fashion Week. Spanning Old Masters and Impressionist masterpieces, the art collection at the Courtauld Gallery is superb.

MORE TO SEE	64

British Library
Charles Dickens Museum
Cleopatra's Needle
Covent Garden Piazza
Eros
Foundling Museum
Handel & Hendrix in London
London Transport Museum
Madame Tussauds

Petrie Museum
Photographers' Gallery
Regent's Park
Sir John Soane's Museum
Wallace Collection
ZSL London Zoo

SHOP 118

Art and Antiques
Grays Antiques Market
Books
Stanfords
Department Stores
Liberty
Selfridges
Fashion
Lulu Guinness
Health and Beauty
Burberry Beauty Box
Neal's Yard Remedies

Homeware
Aram Designs Ltd
Designers Guild
Heal's
Thomas Goode Ltd
Toys
Benjamin Pollock's Toyshop
Hamleys

ENTERTAINMENT 128

Clubs
The Borderline
Salsa!
Opera, Ballet and Concerts
London Coliseum
Royal Opera House
Wigmore Hall

Theaters
Donmar Warehouse
Theatre Royal, Drury Lane

EAT 140

Asian
Benares
Chaopraya Eat-Thai
Masala Zone
Rasa W1
Brasseries/Brunch
Christopher's
Joe Allen
British and Modern
Rules
European
Gaby's Deli
Icebar London
Olivelli

Villandry
Wild Honey
Famous Chefs
The Square
Tom's Kitchen
Gastropubs/Bars
The Dog and Duck
Lowlander Grand Café
International
Ceviche
Vegetarian
Wild Food Café

CITY TOURS

Westminster and St. James's

Westminster Abbey, the Houses of Parliament, Buckingham Palace, Trafalgar Square—some of London's most famous landmarks are located in Westminster. Follow in the footsteps of royalty as you take in famous art galleries, London's prettiest royal park and some upscale shopping.

Morning

Begin your day at **Trafalgar Square** (▷ 75), where Sir Edwin Landseer's lions proudly protect Nelson's Column. Presiding over its northern side, the **National Gallery** (▷ 34–35) shows Western European art in a stately setting. Next door, the **National Portrait Gallery** (above, ▷ 36–37) puts faces to famous names down the centuries. Both galleries have good cafés, but you may also like the nearby **Café in the Crypt** at **St. Martin-in-the-Fields** (▷ 138). Perhaps book for a candlelit concert while you are there.

Mid-morning

Walk down Whitehall to visit the **Banqueting House** (right, ▷ 14–15), noted for its Rubens ceiling, and to see **Horse Guards** and the **Cenotaph** war memorial. You soon arrive at **Big Ben** and the **Houses of Parliament** (▷ 22–23). There are splendid views of the River Thames from Westminster Bridge, immortalized by poet William Wordsworth and Impressionist Claude Monet. **Westminster Abbey** (▷ 62–63) lies across the square.

Lunch

Turn up Storey's Gate to **St. James's Park** (▷ 42–43), perhaps picking up a sandwich en route to eat in this pretty royal park. Alternatively, try **Inn the Park** (▷ 147). You will pass the **Churchill War Rooms** (▷ 67) beneath a sweeping flight of steps, watched over by the statue of an imperious Clive of India, and may wish to return there after lunch. Stroll among the park's trees and flowerbeds and watch the ducks, geese and pelicans feeding on the lake.

Afternoon

Crossing the Mall, a wide ceremonial route packed with crowds on great occasions, you will see **Buckingham Palace** (above, ▷ 18–19) on your left, fronted by the Queen Victoria Memorial. Walk up the Mall to get a closer look at the palace, or cross to Marlborough Road alongside the red-brick **St. James's Palace.** It houses the Household Office of Prince William and Prince Harry. **Clarence House** (▷ 68), official London residence of Prince Charles and the Duchess of Cornwall, is on the far side of the palace.

Mid-afternoon

St. James's Street is lined with old-established businesses and famously exclusive members' clubs. Turn right into Jermyn Street for more quintessentially British shops, many carrying the Royal Warrant. Walking through the elegant Piccadilly Arcade brings you into Piccadilly, where **Fortnum & Mason** (▷ 124) is the perfect place for afternoon tea. **Hatchards** (▷ 125), booksellers since 1797, is next door. Visit **St. James's, Piccadilly** (▷ 73), Wren's church for the local aristocracy. There may be a concert on there in the evening.

Evening

If you like the Grand Café tradition, **The Wolseley** (▷ 151) is for you. Or dress up for a meal at **Tamarind** (▷ 150–151) in Mayfair. As an alternative, reserve an evening **Thames River dinner cruise** (left, ▷ 56–57).

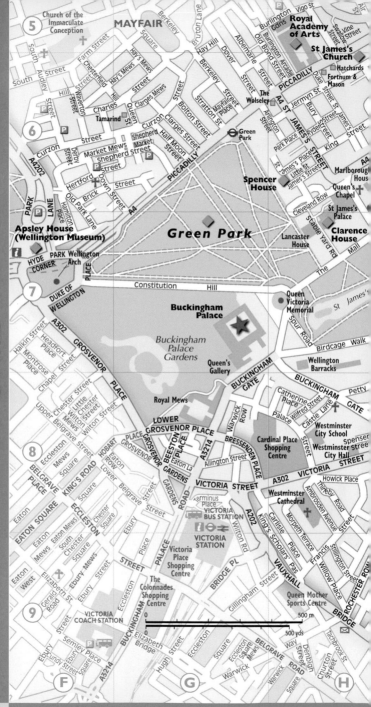

CITY TOURS

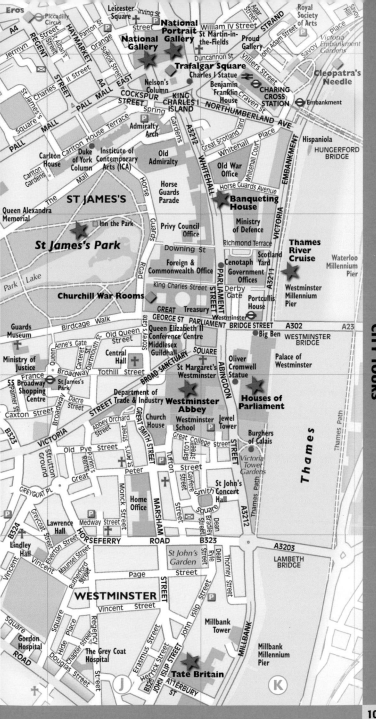

Westminster and St. James's
Quick Reference Guide

SIGHTS AND EXPERIENCES

Banqueting House (▷ 14)
Inigo Jones's 17th-century architectural masterpiece has a magnificent Rubens ceiling.

Buckingham Palace (▷ 18)
The summer opening of this royal residence and office of the Royal Household is not to be missed.

Houses of Parliament (▷ 22)
Britain is governed from this landmark Victorian Gothic building on the banks of the Thames.

National Gallery (▷ 34)
The superb collection gives an overview of European painting from Giotto to Cézanne.

National Portrait Gallery (▷ 36)
The famous and the infamous, past and present, are portrayed in paintings and photographs.

St. James's Park (▷ 42)
Tree-filled, surrounded by palaces and with a lake at its heart, this is the prettiest of the royal parks.

Tate Britain (▷ 52)
Tate Britain exhibits British art from 1500 to the 21st century, with a whole gallery devoted to Turner.

Thames River Cruise (▷ 56)
Sit down, relax and enjoy views of some of the most beautiful and interesting buildings in London.

Westminster Abbey (▷ 62)

The vast abbey is full of exquisite detail and monuments. Herein lies a pageant of British history.

MORE TO SEE 64

Apsley House
Churchill War Rooms
Clarence House
Green Park

Royal Academy of Arts
St. James's, Piccadilly
Spencer House
Trafalgar Square

SHOP 118

Books
Hatchards
Department Stores
Fortnum & Mason

Fashion
Turnbull & Asser
Health and Beauty
Floris

ENTERTAINMENT 128

Comedy
The Comedy Store
Dancing
The Ritz
Film
Institute of Contemporary Arts
  (ICA)

Opera, Ballet and Concerts
St. James's, Piccadilly
St. Martin-in-the-Fields

EAT 140

Asian
Tamarind
British and Modern
Portrait Restaurant
The Wolseley

Lighter Bites
Inn the Park

Around Hyde Park

A feast of world-class museums and music put South Kensington firmly on every visitor's must-see list. Adjoining Hyde Park, Kensington Gardens come complete with a romantic royal palace and memories of Diana, Princess of Wales, who lived there.

CITY TOURS

Morning
At **South Kensington Underground** station there's a passage marked "To the Museums." Follow it, or come up to street level for a fortifying breakfast at one of the many cafés and pâtisseries that crowd this popular area. You are heading for the Cromwell Road and three world-class museums: the **Victoria and Albert Museum** (left, ▷ 60–61), the **Natural History Museum** (▷ 38–39) and the **Science Museum** (▷ 46–47). They are free, so you could pop into each one to get an idea of their riches, or spend the morning engrossed in the subjects that interest you most.

Mid-morning
All three museums have **cafés** to retreat to for sustenance. The café at the V&A is located in what was the world's first museum restaurant, in rooms intended as a showpiece of modern design and craftsmanship. During summer you can eat outdoors. The cafés at the Science and Natural History museums are particularly child-friendly.

Lunch
Walk up Exhibition Road toward **Hyde Park** (▷ 71), turning left at Prince Consort Road to view the stately **Royal College of Music** and to approach the elliptical **Royal Albert Hall** (▷ 137). **Verdi–Italian Kitchen** upstairs is a good lunch spot and you could perhaps make reservations for a concert or tour. Look at the detail on the frieze that rings this distinctive domed building and, going west, don't miss the reliefs and *sgraffito* that decorate the facade of the building opposite, previously occupied by the Royal College of Organists.

Afternoon

Cross Kensington Gore to the **Albert Memorial** (right, ▷ 66), an ornate fantasy in glittering gold by George Gilbert Scott. Stroll through **Kensington Gardens** (▷ 26–27) to the Diana, Princess of Wales Memorial Fountain in adjacent Hyde Park. Then take the path back through Kensington Gardens via the Round Pond to **Kensington Palace** (▷ 26–27).

Mid-afternoon

Tour Kensington Palace and take afternoon tea in **The Orangery** (▷ 148–149). Leaving by the Kensington Palace Gardens exit and "billionaires' row" of embassies, cross Kensington Church Street to the specialist shops and galleries along **Holland Street**. Turn left down **Kensington Church Walk** for exquisite little shops, courtyard houses and gardens. This is a secret, village-like London, yet it's only seconds away from busy Kensington High Street.

Dinner

Babylon (▷ 144), with its rooftop gardens and fabulous views across London, is nearby, as is Kensington favorite **Maggie Jones's** (▷ 148). Or you could take the bus to Knightsbridge, go shopping and relax in the **Champagne Bar** at **Harrods** (below, ▷ 124–125).

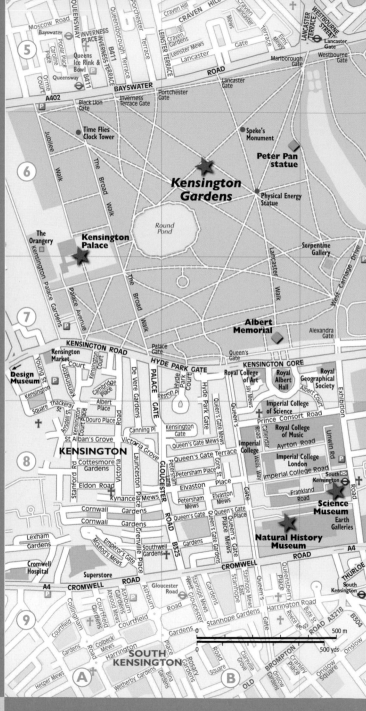

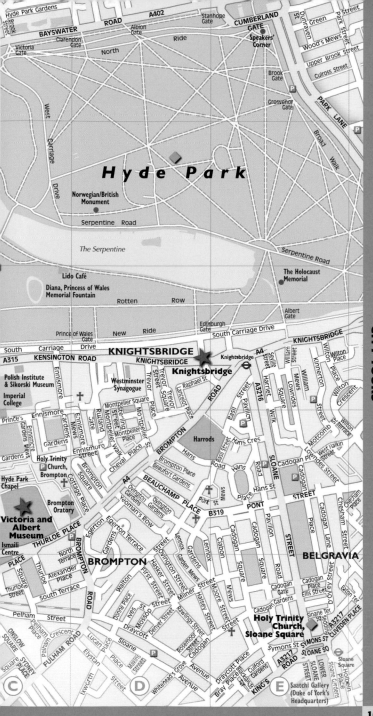

Around Hyde Park
Quick Reference Guide

 SIGHTS AND EXPERIENCES

Kensington Palace and Gardens (▷ 26)

This historic royal residence, set in the beautiful 110ha (272-acre) Kensington Gardens, was once home to Queen Victoria and Diana, Princess of Wales.

Knightsbridge Shopping (▷ 28)

Knightsbridge's shops enthrall the most dedicated fashionista, with window displays to delight the eye. Don't miss those famous London landmarks: Harvey Nichols and Harrods.

Natural History Museum (▷ 38)

With everything that you have ever wanted to know about the natural world and a whole lot more under one roof, the museum is a truly fascinating place.

Science Museum (▷ 46)

With exhibits ranging from Stephenson's steam locomotive *Rocket* to a space capsule, and with an IMAX cinema and plenty of hands-on fun, the museum makes science entertaining.

Victoria and Albert Museum (▷ 60)

This wonderful treasure house of decorative arts, one of the largest collections of its kind in the world, delights, inspires and often surprises.

MORE TO SEE 64

Albert Memorial
Design Museum
Holy Trinity, Sloane Square
Hyde Park
Peter Pan statue

SHOP 118

Art and Antiques
Kensington Church Street
Department Stores
Harrods
Harvey Nichols
Peter Jones

Fashion
Brora
Jimmy Choo

ENTERTAINMENT 128

Film
Ciné Lumière
Opera, Ballet and Concerts
Cadogan Hall
Holland Park Theatre
Royal Albert Hall

Theaters
Royal Court/Jerwood Theatre
  Upstairs

EAT 140

Asian
Amaya
Royal China
British and Modern
Babylon
Bibendum
Maggie Jones's

Famous Chefs
Le Gavroche
Lighter Bites
The Orangery

Farther Afield

Birthplace of Henry VIII and Elizabeth I, home to the National Maritime Museum and famed for the Royal Observatory, Greenwich (▷ 20–21) makes a great escape from central London, with open parkland, river views and a lively market selling food and crafts.

Morning

The perfect way to travel to Greenwich is by boat, as the royals did in centuries past, for the **Old Royal Naval College** (above, ▷ 20) presents a splendid baroque facade to the river. Alternatively, the Docklands Light Railway (DLR) gets you there quickly. Make your first stop the **Discover Greenwich** tourist information center, which has an excellent exhibition on the **Maritime Greenwich World Heritage Site** and the very good **Old Brewery** café/bar (tel 020 3437 2222). Located in the Pepys Building, it is close to the magnificent *Cutty Sark*, the world's last tea clipper, restored after serious fire damage.

Mid-morning

Cross Romney Road to visit the **National Maritime Museum** (right, ▷ 21) and delve into all matters nautical, with plenty of hands-on exhibits. A colonnade links the museum with the elegant Palladian-style **Queen's House**, designed by Inigo Jones in the 17th-century. Today it houses a fine art collection with works by Gainsborough, Reynolds and Turner. Back across Romney Road, visit the neo-classical **Chapel of St. Peter and St. Paul** and the magnificent **Painted Hall** of the Old Royal Naval College. The ceiling here took 19 years to complete and the artist, James Thornhill, was eventually knighted for his labors. It was here that the body of Admiral Lord Nelson lay in state after the Battle of Trafalgar.

CITY TOURS

Lunch

There's a good **restaurant** downstairs in the Old Royal Naval College, or for something less formal you could choose to return to the **Old Brewery** in the Pepys Building.

Afternoon

Now head up the hill in Greenwich Park to the **Royal Observatory** (above, ▷ 21), commissioned by Charles II and designed by Wren in 1675 with the purpose of finding longitude at sea. The Time galleries' exhibits, interactive **Astronomy Centre** and the **Peter Harrison Planetarium** are fascinating. Here you can stand astride the **Greenwich Meridian** line.

Mid-afternoon

Covering 74ha (183 acres) **Greenwich Park** is the oldest enclosed royal park, with rose gardens, a flower garden, lake, wilderness deer park and fine views across the Thames to Docklands and the City of London (left). Follow a path leading to Regency houses on Crooms Hill and continue downhill to the lively weekend **market**, packed with food stalls, crafts and small design shops.

Dinner

Take the DLR to **Canary Wharf** (▷ 76), in the heart of Docklands, to eat at the 18th-century waterside pub **The Gun** (▷ 147), once the haunt of smugglers and Lord Nelson's favorite trysting place.

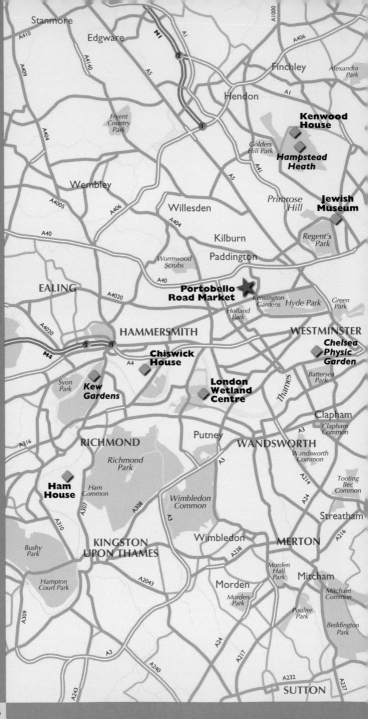

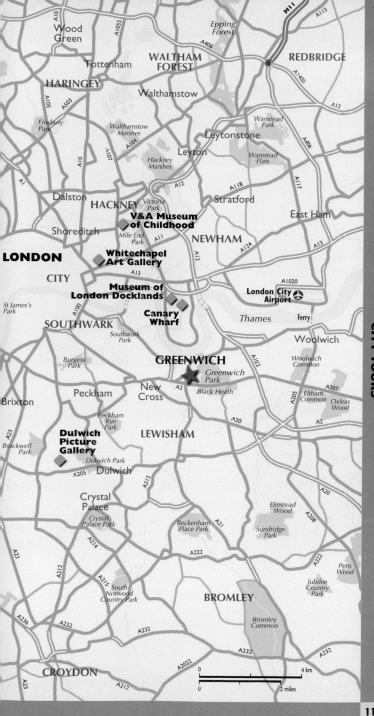

Wood Green

Tottenham

HARINGEY

Finsbury
Park

Dalston

Shoreditch

LONDON

CITY

St James's
Park

SOUTHWARK

Brixton

Peckham

Burgess
Park

Brockwell
Park

**Dulwich
Picture
Gallery**

Crystal
Palace

Crystal
Palace Park

WALTHAM
FOREST

Walthamstow

Walthamstow
Marshes

Hackney
Marshes

HACKNEY

Victoria
Park

**V&A Museum
of Childhood**

Mile End
Park

**Whitechapel
Art Gallery**

**Museum of
London Docklands**

**Canary
Wharf**

Southwark
Park

Peckham
Rye
Park

LEWISHAM

Dulwich Park

Dulwich

A205

South
Norwood
Country Park

CROYDON

Epping
Forest

M11

REDBRIDGE

Leytonstone

Wanstead
Park

Leyton

Wanstead
Flats

Stratford

East Ham

NEWHAM

**London City
Airport**

Thames

Ferry

Woolwich

GREENWICH

Greenwich
Park

Black Heath

New
Cross

A2

Woolwich
Common

Eltham
Common

Oxleas
Wood

Peckham
Rye
Park

Elmstead
Wood

Sundridge
Park

Beckenham
Place Park

BROMLEY

Bromley
Common

Jubilee
Country
Park

Petts
Wood

0   4 km

0   2 miles

SIGHTS AND EXPERIENCES

Greenwich (▷ 20)

The ideal way to spend a Sunday is to take a cruise on the Thames to Greenwich, a UNESCO World Heritage Site. Visit the great maritime sights and the Royal Observatory, take a leisurely stroll in historic Greenwich Park and shop in the lively crafts market.

Portobello Road Market (▷ 40)

Dedicate a Saturday to exploring the shops and stalls of an antiques market like no other. Whatever you're looking for, be it glass, china, curios or jewelry, it's likely you'll find it here, and searching for treasure and bargaining with the dealers is all part of the fun.

CITY TOURS

MORE TO SEE	64

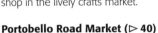

Canary Wharf
Chelsea Physic Garden
Chiswick House
Dulwich Picture Gallery
Ham House
Hampstead Heath
Jewish Museum

Kenwood House
Kew Gardens
London Wetland Centre
Museum of London Docklands
V&A Museum of Childhood
Whitechapel Art Gallery

SHOP 118

Books
Books for Cooks
Homeware
Contemporary Applied Arts
Shopping Centers
Westfield London

Street Markets
Camden Markets

ENTERTAINMENT 128

Cabaret
The Pheasantry, Chelsea
Clubs
606 Club
Bush Hall
Koko
O2 Academy Brixton
The Pheasantry, Chelsea
Events
O2 Arena
Jazz
Bull's Head, Barnes
The Jazz Café

Opera, Ballet and Concerts
Roundhouse
Sadler's Wells Theatre
Wilton's Music Hall
Sport
All England Lawn Tennis Club,
 Wimbledon
Kia Oval
Lord's Cricket Ground
Wembley

EAT 140

British and Modern
The Glasshouse
Grainstore
Medlar
European
Ottolenghi
La Poule au Pot
Providores & Tapa Room

Gastropubs/Bars
The Gun

Shop

Whether you're looking for the best local products, a department store or a quirky boutique, you'll find them all in London. In this section shops are listed alphabetically.

Introduction	**120**
Directory	**122**
Shopping A–Z	**123**

SHOP

Introduction

If England is a nation of shop-keepers, then London is the head office. You can find almost anything if you are determined enough. London has long been the world's marketplace and you'll find saris and spices as easily as rare reggae records, depending on the district—it really pays to explore beyond the West End. For shoppers, the choice ranges from vibrant street markets to legendary department stores and from offbeat boutiques to smart galleries of paintings and antiques.

Contemporary and Traditional

It is the extraordinary range that excites visitors. London has outrageous fashion, bolstered by the annual crop of imaginative art-, fashion- and design-school graduates. By contrast, long-established shopping streets, such as Oxford Street and Kensington High Street, offer mass-market goods, while markets such as Camden Lock and Portobello Road are eclectic, ethnic and inexpensive.

Buying a London Memory

London's souvenirs range from tatty to tasteful. Ever since the Swinging Sixties, anything with a Union Jack flag on it has sold well. For high

BEST OF BRITISH

Take home some British souvenirs with a difference. You can buy beautifully crafted umbrellas and walking sticks from James Smith & Sons (✉ 53 New Oxford Street, WC1). For a good British cheese buy a Stilton, all ready and packed, from Paxton & Whitfield (✉ 93 Jermyn Street, SW1). If you want to try some British recipes go to Books for Cooks (✉ 4 Blenheim Crescent, W11) for a large selection of cookbooks. Tea addicts should head to The Tea House (✉ 15 Neal Street, WC2) for a choice of blends and some stylish teapots. For bespoke stationery and leather goods, Smythson (✉ 40 New Bond Street, W1) is the epitome of elegance.

Clockwise from top: The elegant arcades of Leadenhall Market; handmade shoes for sale in St. James's; one of the antiques shops in Camden Passage; the central well

quality, go to the museum shops. Gifts at the shop in Buckingham Palace Mews include the Queen Victoria range of china, a mini-crown for a charm bracelet or a guardsman mug. The Victoria and Albert Museum, British Museum and National Gallery also stock quality items inspired by their diverse collections—budget permitting, you can do a full-scale family gift shop at any of these. Tate Modern has fine handcrafted jewelry, while the Museum of London is particularly good for souvenirs and books about London. At the National Portrait Gallery, you will find books on historical figures and British history, as well as a good supply of postcards and posters.

The Ultimate British Buy

Go to St. James's or Knightsbridge to purchase traditional British-made goods such as tweed jackets, handmade shoes or elegant china, delicate fragrances, floral-printed fabrics and cashmere sweaters. Visit Burlington Arcade (▷ panel below) for its specialist upscale shops in a historic setting. Burberry and Aquascutum are synonymous with raincoats. Harrods has been trading for some 150 years; Selfridges was the country's first department store and is the second largest after Harrods; and Liberty fabrics are still exotic and luxurious. The winter and summer sales are major events in any serious shopper's diary.

SHOP

SHOP THE SHOP

Charles Dickens would recognize many London shops. Burlington Arcade, off Piccadilly, is an 18th-century covered shopping mall, with a liveried beadle to maintain decorum. Many shops display the royal insignia, showing that they supply members of the Royal Household with everything from brushes to jewels (royalwarrant.org). For instance, John Lobb (✉ 9 St. James's Street, SW1) custom-makes shoes and boots for the royal family—and for you, at a price.

in Liberty; Lobb on St. James's Street, selling exclusive made-to-measure shoes; Fortnum & Mason in Piccadilly, renowned for its luxury foods and top notch wines

Directory

Fleet Street to the Tower

Fashion
The Goodhood Store
Luna & Curious
Food and Drink
Paul
Shopping Centers
Royal Exchange
Street Markets
Leadenhall Market

Covent Garden to Regent's Park

Art and Antiques
Grays Antiques Market
Books
Stanfords
Department Stores
Liberty
Selfridges
Fashion
Lulu Guinness
Health and Beauty
Burberry Beauty Box
Neal's Yard Remedies
Homeware
Aram Designs Ltd
Designers Guild
Heal's
Thomas Goode Ltd
Toys
Benjamin Pollock's Toyshop
Hamleys

Westminster and St. James's

Books
Hatchards
Department Stores
Fortnum & Mason
Fashion
Turnbull & Asser
Health and Beauty
Floris

Around Hyde Park

Department Stores
Harrods
Harvey Nichols
Peter Jones
Fashion
Brora
Jimmy Choo

Farther Afield

Books
Books for Cooks
Homeware
Contemporary Applied Arts
Shopping Centers
Westfield London
Street Markets
Camden Markets

Shopping A–Z

ARAM DESIGNS LTD

aram.co.uk

Displayed over five floors, the latest, most innovative designs in top-quality furniture and lighting can be seen here, created by internationally renowned designers and talented new graduates from all areas of the applied arts.

➕ L4 ✉ 110 Drury Lane, WC2 ☎ 020 7557 7557 🕐 Mon–Sat 10–6 (Thu until 7) 🚇 Covent Garden

BENJAMIN POLLOCK'S TOYSHOP

pollocks-coventgarden.co.uk

Selling traditional toy theaters, paper models, puppets, music boxes and all kinds of collectible toys for children and adults, this shop is delightfully different.

➕ K5 ✉ 44 The Market, WC2 ☎ 020 7379 7866 🕐 Mon–Wed 10.30–6, Thu–Sat 10.30–6.30, Sun 11–6 🚇 Covent Garden

BOOKS FOR COOKS

booksforcooks.com

Browse the amazing selection of books about cooking and cuisine, then head to the café, where recipes are tested. Classes are held in the demonstration kitchen.

➕ Off map ✉ 4 Blenheim Crescent, W11 ☎ 020 7221 1992 🕐 Tue–Sat 10–6. Closed last 3 weeks in Aug 🚇 Ladbroke Grove

BRORA

brora.co.uk

Choose from cashmere in an array of rich and subtle shades for men, women and children. Plain or patterned, it is expensive, but the quality is superb.

➕ E9 ✉ 6–8 Symons Street, SW3 ☎ 020 7730 2665 🕐 Mon–Tue, Sat 10–6, Wed–Fri 10–7, Sun 12–5 🚇 Sloane Square

BURBERRY BEAUTY BOX

uk.burberry.com

The iconic British brand's latest concept store features make-up, fragrances and fashion in eye-catching displays and digital innovations. Mix, match and box up your favorites at the Beauty Box Bar and maybe opt for a personal beauty consultation.

➕ K5 ✉ 3a The Market Building, Covent Garden, WC2 ☎ 020 3425 7020 🕐 Mon–Sat 10–8, Sun 12–6 🚇 Covent Garden

CAMDEN MARKETS

camdenmarket.com

Source of all things funky and fun, with an eclectic mix of stores and stalls, this is the place to head for vintage clothing and design, futuristic clubwear, tribal jewelry, reggae records, handmade accessories and alternative gifts, plus street food, bars and cult cafés. It's at its height on the weekend.

➕ Off map ✉ Camden Lock Place, NW1 🕐 Daily 10–late; times vary for each business 🚇 Camden Town, Chalk Farm

CONTEMPORARY APPLIED ARTS

caa.org.uk

Dedicated to promoting British artists, the CAA shop displays outstanding contemporary crafts, from

ceramics, glass and textiles to jewelry, metalwork and wood.
➕ N6 ✉ 89 Southwark Street, SE1 ☎ 020 7620 0086 ◉ Mon–Sat 10–6 🚇 Southwark, Blackfriars

DESIGNERS GUILD
designersguild.com
Tricia Guild's store is a wonderland of exquisite design, with a range of modern china, glass and fabrics.
➕ F3 ✉ 76 Marylebone High Street, W1 ☎ 020 3301 5826 ◉ Mon–Sat 10–6 (Thu until 7), Sun 11–5 🚇 Baker Street

FLORIS
florislondon.com
Creating gorgeous fragrances since 1730, this original shop, still run by the founder's descendents, has oak-paneled counters and a sense of history and tradition. Deliciously scented candles are a luxurious treat for the home.
➕ H6 ✉ 89 Jermyn Street, SW1 ☎ 020 7747 3612 ◉ Mon–Fri 9.30–6.30 (Thu till 7), Sat 10–7 🚇 Green Park, Piccadilly Circus

FORTNUM & MASON
fortnumandmason.com
Before venturing into London's premier grocer's shop, do not miss the clock, which has Messrs. Fortnum and Mason edging forward each hour. The shop-brand Fortnum's goods make perfectly delicious presents.
➕ H6 ✉ 181 Piccadilly, W1 ☎ 020 7734 8040 ◉ Mon–Sat 10–9, Sun 12–6 🚇 Piccadilly Circus, Green Park

THE GOODHOOD STORE
goodhoodstore.com
This award-winning retailer sells more than 200 brands, spanning menswear, womenswear, lifestyle and beauty. The emphasis is on contemporary style and luxury.
➕ R1 ✉ 151 Curtain Road, EC2 ☎ 020 7729 3600 ◉ Mon–Fri 10.30–6.30, Sat 10.30–7, Sun 12–6 🚇 Old Street

GRAYS ANTIQUES MARKET
graysantiques.com
In two labyrinthine buildings, over 200 dealers sell antiques, fine jewelry and vintage collectibles in a diverse mix that includes objets d'art, silver, textiles and timepieces.
➕ F5 ✉ 1–7 Davies Mews and 58 Davies Street, W1 ☎ 020 7629 7034 ◉ Mon–Fri 10–6, Sat 11–5 🚇 Bond Street

HAMLEYS
hamleys.com
In business for more than 250 years and probably the world's most famous toy shop, Hamleys has five action-packed floors.
➕ H5 ✉ 188–196 Regent Street, W1 ☎ 0371 704 1977 ◉ Mon–Wed 10–8, Thu–Fri 10–9, Sat 9.30–9, Sun 12–6 🚇 Oxford Circus

HARRODS
harrods.com
This vast emporium contains just about everything anyone could want. Don't miss the food halls.

D8 ✉ 87–135 Brompton Road, SW1 ☎ 020 7730 1234 🕐 Mon–Sat 10–9, Sun 11.30–6 🚇 Knightsbridge

HARVEY NICHOLS

harveynichols.com

Designer fashion, decadent jewelry, exclusive beauty, luxury food and drink—elegance and style are assured in the store that bags the title London's classiest clothes shop. It also has a popular restaurant.

E7 ✉ 109–125 Knightsbridge, SW1 ☎ 020 7235 5000 🕐 Mon–Sat 10–8, Sun 11.30–6 🚇 Knightsbridge

HATCHARDS

hatchards.co.uk

Booksellers since 1797, Hatchards is the oldest bookshop in London and is still in its original building.

H6 ✉ 187 Piccadilly, W1 ☎ 020 7439 9921 🕐 Mon–Sat 9.30–8, Sun 12–6.30 🚇 Piccadilly Circus, Green Park

HEAL'S

heals.com

First opened in 1854 and a front-runner of the 1920s Arts and Crafts movement, Heal's specializes in timeless, modern designer furniture and homewares.

H3 ✉ 196 Tottenham Court Road, W1 ☎ 020 7636 1666 🕐 Mon–Sat 10–7, Thu 10–8, Sun 12–6 🚇 Goodge Street

AUCTION HOUSES

A visit to one of London's auction houses, even just to view, is an experience. Try Bonham's (✉ 101 New Bond Street, W1 ☎ 020 7447 7447, bonhams.com), Christie's (✉ 8 King Street, SW1 ☎ 020 7839 9060, christies.com) or Sotheby's (✉ 34 New Bond Street, W1 ☎ 020 7293 5000, sothebys.com).

JIMMY CHOO

jimmychoo.com

A fashionista heaven, Jimmy Choo in Knightsbridge is the place to buy the highest-heeled shoes in the latest styles in town.

E8 ✉ 32 Sloane Street, SW3 ☎ 020 7823 1051 🕐 Mon–Sat 10–7, Sun 12–5 🚇 Knightsbridge

LEADENHALL MARKET

cityoflondon.gov.uk

This surprising City treat is housed under Sir Horace Jones's magnificent 19th-century wrought-iron and glass arcades. Quality food shops, boutiques, pubs and restaurants sit behind the traditional shop fronts on cobbled streets.

Vibrant Camden Lock Market

MAKE A PICNIC

With so many parks and benches, London is a great place to picnic. The big stores have seductive food halls and stock wine; see Harrods, Selfridges and Fortnum & Mason. Old Compton Street is a food shopper's delight; see also Villandry (✉ 170 Great Portland Street, W1) for a feast of salads, pastas, fresh juices and delicious cakes and tarts.

➕ R4 ✉ Leadenhall, EC3 🕐 Mon–Fri 10–6. Individual shops may differ 🚇 Bank, Monument

LIBERTY

libertylondon.com

With everything from sumptuous fabrics to china and glass, this shop is characterized by exoticism and cutting-edge fashion, with an Arts and Crafts heritage.

➕ G4 ✉ Regent Street, W1 ☎ 020 7734 1234 🕐 Mon–Sat 10–8, Sun 12–6 🚇 Oxford Circus

LULU GUINNESS

luluguinness.com

Celebrities and wannabees love designer Lulu Guinness's distinctive bags and accessories, many featuring her signature lips motif.

➕ K5 ✉ 9 The Piazza, Covent Garden, WC2 ☎ 020 7240 2537 🕐 Mon–Sat 10–7, Sun 11–5 🚇 Covent Garden

LUNA & CURIOUS

lunaandcurious.com

Some of London's most innovative shops are in Shoreditch (▷ 6–7) and this creative hub is well worth seeking out for fashion, jewelry, accessories and homewares.

➕ S2 ✉ 24–26 Calvert Avenue, E2 ☎ 020 3222 0034 🕐 Mon–Sat 11–6, Sun 11–5 🚇 Old Street

NEAL'S YARD REMEDIES

nealsyardremedies.com

Believing in "beauty with no nasties," Neal's Yard specializes in organic, plant-based cosmetics and skincare products, herbal remedies and aromatherapy oils.

➕ K4 ✉ 15 Neal's Yard, WC2 ☎ 020 7379 7222 🕐 Mon–Sat 10–8, Sun 10–6.30 🚇 Covent Garden

PAUL

paul-uk.com

This iconic French bakery offers a tempting array of filled baguettes and salads, which you can eat at the tables outside, as well as traditional breads and tarts.

➕ N4 ✉ 2 Paternoster Square, EC4 ☎ 020 7329 4705 🕐 Mon–Fri 7–7, Sat–Sun 8–7 🚇 St. Paul's

PETER JONES

johnlewis.com

This department store sells everything from designer fashion to homewares, and offers great views from the café and cocktail bar.

➕ E9 ✉ Sloane Square, SW1 ☎ 020 7730 3434 🕐 Mon–Sat 9.30–7 (Wed until 8), Sun 12–6 🚇 Sloane Square

ROYAL EXCHANGE

theroyalexchange.co.uk

William Tite's City landmark is now a beautiful shopping mall, where boutiques stock luxury gifts, watches, jewelry, fine art, handcrafted leather goods, stationery and designer fashion, and the dining options are equally stylish.

➕ Q4 ✉ Cornhill ☎ 020 7283 8935 🕐 For individual stores see website; restaurants and bars 8am–11pm 🚇 Bank

SELFRIDGES

selfridges.com

You could spend a whole day in this flagship store, where every department has eye appeal, from the fashion floors to the superb food hall, and the restaurants and cafés are memorable.

➕ F4 ✉ 400 Oxford Street, W1 ☎ 0800 123 400 🕐 Mon–Sat 9.30–9, Sun 11.30–6 Ⓢ Marble Arch, Bond Street

STANFORDS

stanfords.co.uk

In business since 1853 and in the same location on Long Acre since 1901, the world's largest map retailer has a vast selection of travel guides and books, along with globes, children's books and toys, gifts, stationery and travel accessories, plus a good little café. This is a must-visit for travel enthusiasts.

➕ K5 ✉ 12–14 Long Acre, WC2 ☎ 020 7836 1321 🕐 Mon–Sat 9–8, Sun 11.30–6 Ⓢ Covent Garden, Leicester Sqaure

THOMAS GOODE LTD

thomasgoode.com

Collectors of bone china, fine glassware and cutlery need look no farther than this splendid showroom. Styles range from contemporary and classic to ultimate luxury.

➕ F6 ✉ 19 South Audley Street, W1 ☎ 020 7499 2823 🕐 Mon–Sat 10–6 Ⓢ Green Park, Bond Street

TURNBULL & ASSER

turnbullandasser.co.uk

If you want classic British design, then the made-to-measure or off-the-peg men's shirts here are for you. The range is complemented by ties and accessories. Quality and service are superb.

➕ H6 ✉ 71–72 Jermyn Street, SW1 ☎ 020 7808 3000 🕐 Mon–Fri 9–6, Sat 9.30–6 Ⓢ Green Park, Piccadilly Circus

WESTFIELD LONDON

uk.westfield.com/london

Westfield has more than 300 shops (spanning designer and high-street labels, department stores and boutiques), restaurants and a multiplex cinema. The larger Westfield Stratford City is located by the Olympic site.

➕ Off map ✉ Ariel Way, W12 ☎ 020 7061 1400 🕐 Mon–Sat 10–10, Sun 12–6 (some stores may vary) Ⓢ Shepherd's Bush, Wood Lane

Liberty's mock-Tudor main entrance

Entertainment

Once you've done with sightseeing for the day, you'll find lots of other great things to do with your time in this chapter, even if all you want to do is relax with a drink. In this section establishments are listed alphabetically.

Introduction   **130**

Directory   **132**

Entertainment A–Z   **133**

ENTERTAINMENT

Introduction

When darkness falls, London's pace doesn't let up, and there's a huge choice of lively nightclubs, bars and pubs where you can mingle with the locals.

Entertainment

London's Theatreland, with its lavish West End musicals and plays starring A-list actors, is famed worldwide, but there's a great deal happening in smaller venues all over town, including alternative theater, comedy and cabaret. Hundreds of concerts take place every week in a variety of buildings, but especially churches, such as St. Martin-in-the-Fields, where the quality of lunchtime and evening recitals is very high and admission is nominal or free. London's newest cultural landmark is King's Place (tel 020 7520 1490, kingsplace.co.uk) in the revitalized area of King's Cross. There are opera, ballet and modern dance seasons in memorable locations, too, plus an array of fun festivals, especially during the summer months and the long public holiday weekends.

Film

As well as the big-screen cinemas in the West End showing the latest blockbuster movies, London has some very good venues screening art-house and indie films. The BFI Southbank

---

WALK THE WALK

The 2km-long (1 mile) stretch of riverside on the South Bank between Westminster Bridge and London Bridge bustles by night, as well as by day. The London Eye is magical after dusk. On the opposite bank, illuminated landmarks include the Houses of Parliament and Somerset House. At Oxo Tower Wharf, go to the top floor for a drink or a meal—there are few better views of London. Admire the Tate Modern (open until 10pm Friday and Saturday) and the Globe, then rest your feet at a riverside pub and enjoy spectacular views.

Clockwise from top: The Garrick Theatre in the West End; the Theatre Royal on Haymarket; the BFI IMAX on the South Bank; Shakespeare's Globe, a re-creation of

(▷ 133), which hosts the annual London Film Festival in October, Ciné Lumière (▷ 134), the Electric Cinema in Notting Hill (electriccinema.co.uk), the Curzon Mayfair and Curzon Bloomsbury (both curzoncinemas.com) are all well worth visiting.

Summer Living

In the summer, London's outdoors comes into its own. Londoners enjoy concerts in beautiful settings such as Hampton Court Palace, Kenwood House, Hyde Park and Kew Gardens, often bringing picnics with them. The music ranges from classical and opera to jazz and rock. Bars, pubs and cafés spill onto the city's streets, and many serve good food.

Clubs, Pubs and Bars

Year-round, the diversity of the club scene is legendary, with many changing themes; check what's on before you go. There are tried-and-tested venues and a host of pulsing new wave options. London's extensive bar scene ranges from cocktails at the elegant Savoy (▷ 159) or the see-and-be-seen Blue Bar at The Berkeley (▷ 156) to Irish bars, sports bars and traditional street-corner pubs. You'll find some are in warrens of Tudor rooms; others take pride in their authentic Victorian and Edwardian decorations.

LANDMARK CLUBBING

A mix of global names, trailblazing bands and DJs make Xoyo (✉ 32–37 Cowper Street, EC2 ☎ 020 7608 2878, xoyo.co.uk) a popular Shoreditch venue. The Nest (✉ 36–44 Stoke Newington Road, N16, ilovethenest.com) promises a soundtrack that covers everything from house and garage to disco, techno and trap from cutting-edge new talent. Under Blackfriars Bridge, Pulse (✉ Invicta Plaza, SE1 ☎ 020 7261 0981, pulseclub.co.uk) is London's largest state-of-the-art club space, with hi-tech sound and video mapping.

an Elizabethan playhouse; Young Dancer, *a bronze by Enzo Plazzotta outside the Royal Opera House in Covent Garden*

ENTERTAINMENT

Directory

South Bank

Clubs
Ministry of Sound
Film
BFI IMAX
BFI Southbank
Opera, Ballet and Concerts
Purcell Room
Queen Elizabeth Hall
Royal Festival Hall
Theaters
National Theatre
Old Vic
Shakespeare's Globe
Young Vic

Fleet Street to the Tower

Clubs
Fabric
Opera, Ballet and Concerts
Barbican Centre
Theaters
Barbican Centre

Covent Garden to Regent's Park

Clubs
The Borderline
Salsa!
Opera, Ballet and Concerts
London Coliseum
Royal Opera House
Wigmore Hall
Theaters
Donmar Warehouse
Theatre Royal, Drury Lane

Westminster to St. James's

Comedy
The Comedy Store
Dancing
The Ritz
Film
Institute of Contemporary Arts (ICA)
Opera, Ballet and Concerts
St. James's, Piccadilly
St. Martin-in-the-Fields

Around Hyde Park

Film
Ciné Lumière
Opera, Ballet and Concerts
Cadogan Hall
Holland Park Theatre
Royal Albert Hall
Theaters
Royal Court/Jerwood Theatre Upstairs

Farther Afield

Cabaret
The Pheasantry, Chelsea
Clubs
606 Club
Bush Hall
Koko
O2 Academy Brixton

Events
O2 Arena

Jazz
Bull's Head, Barnes
The Jazz Café
Opera, Ballet and Concerts
Roundhouse
Sadler's Wells Theatre
Wilton's Music Hall
Sport
All England Lawn Tennis Club, Wimbledon
Kia Oval
Lord's Cricket Ground
Wembley

Entertainment A–Z

606 CLUB

606club.co.uk

West London's best small jazz club books British-based musicians with impeccable credentials. Alcohol is served only with food and the music cover charge is added to the cost of the meal.

➕ Off map ✉ 90 Lots Road, SW10 ☎ 020 7352 5953 🕐 Mon–Thu 7pm–1am, Fri–Sat 8pm–2am, Sun 7–11pm (plus regular Sunday lunches) 🚇 Earl's Court then bus C3, Fulham Broadway

ALL ENGLAND LAWN TENNIS CLUB, WIMBLEDON

wimbledon.com

In late June, line up for tickets to tennis's top tournament (advance tickets only for the last four days). Tours and museum entrance are available all year.

➕ Off map ✉ Church Road, SW19 ☎ Tours: 020 8946 6131 🚇 Southfields

BARBICAN CENTRE

barbican.org.uk

At Europe's largest multi-arts venue, world-famous orchestras and singers appear in the concert hall, while the theatre stages innovative plays and dance productions. The Barbican also hosts film screenings, festivals, art exhibitions, talks and events, with plentiful venues to eat and drink.

➕ P3 ✉ Barbican Centre, Silk Street, EC2 ☎ 020 7638 8891 🚇 Barbican

BFI IMAX

bfi.org.uk/bfi-imax

Watch exhilarating 2D and 3D movies on the biggest screen in Britain in this 500-seat cinema in a space-age setting.

➕ L6 ✉ 1 Charlie Chaplin Walk, South Bank, SE1 ☎ 0330 333 7878 🚇 Waterloo

BFI SOUTHBANK

whatson.bfi.org.uk

See classic and new movies at this four screen cinema famed for its seasons, festivals, events, previews and director and actor retrospectives. Eat and drink while enjoying riverside views. Some discounted tickets are usually available.

➕ L6 ✉ South Bank, SE1 ☎ 020 7928 3232 🕐 Daily 9.45am–11pm 🚇 Waterloo

THE BORDERLINE

theborderlinelondon.com

The hottest indie and rock bands strut their stuff at the venerable Borderline club in the West End.

➕ J4 ✉ Orange Yard, off Manette Street, W1 ☎ 020 7734 5547 🕐 Concerts: 7–11pm. Clubs and special events 11pm–3 or 4am 🚇 Tottenham Court Road

BULL'S HEAD, BARNES

thebullsheadbarnes.com

This cozy riverside pub serves good food and live music nightly and some Sunday lunchtimes—mainly jazz, but check the website to see who is playing and when.

➕ Off map ✉ 373 Lonsdale Road, SW13 ☎ 020 8876 5241 🕐 Mon–Fri 11am–11pm, Sat 12–11, Sun 12–10; jazz nightly from 7–11pm 🚇 Barnes Bridge

---

THEATER TIPS

If you care about where you sit, you can usually find a seating plan online. For an evening "sold out" performance, it is worth waiting in line for returns; otherwise, try for a matinée. The cheapest seats may be far from the stage, uncomfortable or have a restricted view, so take binoculars and a cushion. Londoners rarely dress up for the theater but they do order their intermission drinks before the play starts.

The famed Comedy Store

BUSH HALL

bushhallmusic.co.uk

Listen to jazz, rock, folk or classics performed by famous names and upcoming artists at this ornate Edwardian dance hall with a rock 'n' roll history as a rehearsal space for the likes of The Who and Adam Faith in the 1960s.

✚ Off map ✉ 310 Uxbridge Road, Shepherd's Bush, W12 ☎ 020 8222 6955 ⏱ Shows: 7.30pm; see website for listings 🚇 Shepherd's Bush Market

CADOGAN HALL

cadoganhall.com

The Royal Philharmonic is the resident orchestra at this excellent venue that attracts international touring orchestras as well as staging contemporary folk, jazz and world music concerts, talks and events. The hall is home to the BBC Proms Chamber Music series.

✚ E9 ✉ 5 Sloane Terrace, SW1 ☎ 020 7730 4500 🚇 Sloane Square

CINÉ LUMIÈRE

institut-francais.org.uk/cine-lumiere/

Part of the French government's hub of language and culture, Ciné Lumière shows French films as well as other European and world cinema.

✚ B9 ✉ Institut Français, 17 Queensberry Place, SW7 ☎ 020 7871 3515 ⏱ Daily 10–9.30. Closed Aug 🚇 South Kensington

THE COMEDY STORE

thecomedystore.co.uk

The best in stand-up comedy features improvised sketches from the Comedy Store Players; sharp, topical comedy from the Cutting Edge team and visiting talent from around the globe. Many big names in British TV and radio have started out here.

✚ J5 ✉ 1a Oxendon Street, SW1 ⏱ Doors open Tue–Thu at 6.30pm, Fri–Sun 6pm. Show times vary 🚇 Piccadilly Circus, Leicester Square

DONMAR WAREHOUSE

donmarwarehouse.com

Awards continue to flood in for this theater with just 250 bench-style seats and a record of innovative productions, from Shakespeare to notable new writing.

➕ K4 ✉ 41 Earlham Street, WC2 🕓 Theater open 10.30–7.30; show times vary 🚇 Covent Garden

FABRIC

fabriclondon.com

This hugely popular superclub has three rooms—two with stages for live acts—dedicated to cutting-edge house, techno, electronica and bass-driven dance music.

➕ N3 ✉ 77a Charterhouse Street, EC1 ☎ 020 7336 8898 🕓 Fri–Sun from 11pm 🚇 Farringdon

HOLLAND PARK THEATRE

operahollandpark.com

Confusingly, highly acclaimed opera, not theater, is staged here in summer (June–July) beneath a temporary canopy sheltering an auditorium of 1,000 seats in one of London's most romantic parks.

➕ Off map ✉ Holland Park, W8 ☎ 0300 999 1000 🚇 Holland Park, High Street Kensington

INSTITUTE OF CONTEMPORARY ARTS (ICA)

ica.org.uk

The Institute of Contemporary Arts hosts cutting-edge art, screens seriously arty films and plays host to performance artists charting new territory in all media.

➕ J6 ✉ The Mall, SW1 ☎ 020 7930 3647 🕓 Tue–Sun 11–11; exhibitions 11–6, Thu 11–9 🚇 Piccadilly Circus, Charing Cross

THE JAZZ CAFÉ

thejazzcafelondon.com

Buzzing nightly with jazz, soul, R&B or funk, this venue in Camden has a mezzanine restaurant with great views of the live show.

➕ Off map ✉ 5 Parkway, NW1 ☎ 020 7485 6834 🕓 Mon–Sun 7pm–2am, club nights until 3 🚇 Camden Town

KIA OVAL

kiaoval.com

Home to Surrey County Cricket Club, The Oval was the first ground in England to host international Test cricket, and in 2017 it hosted its 100th Test Match. Watch county matches and world stars in action here or join a tour of the ground (not on match days).

➕ Off map ✉ Surrey County Cricket Club, Kennington, SE11 🚇 Oval

KOKO

koko.uk.com

Since 1890, this Camden Town venue has been through many incarnations. Today, go for hip-hop, trance, pop, rock and partying under the gigantic mirror ball.

➕ Off map ✉ 1a Camden High Street, NW1 ☎ 020 7388 3222 🕓 Sun–Thu 7pm–11.30pm, Fri 7pm–10pm. Club NME: Fri–Sat 10pm–4am 🚇 Mornington Crescent, Camden Town

LONDON COLISEUM

eno.org

London's largest theater (over 2,300 seats) is home to the English National Opera (ENO). All operas here are sung in English.

ALL THAT JAZZ

London has a great concentration of world-class jazz musicians—home-grown and foreign, traditional and contemporary. Evening and late-night gigs cover rock, roots, rhythm and blues and more, many in pubs. For a list of venues, check *Time Out* magazine. Also, to get the latest information on jazz visit jazznights.co.uk.

The English National Ballet and other renowned dance companies take to the stage during breaks in ENO seasons. Guided tours reveal the detail of this beautifully restored Edwardian theater.

🚇 K5 ✉ St. Martin's Lane, WC2
☎ 020 7845 9300 Ⓔ Leicester Square, Charing Cross

LORD'S CRICKET GROUND

lords.org

Lord's is the home of Marylebone Cricket Club, and is where Middlesex play home games. The ground hosts test cricket, major finals and Sunday league games.

🚇 Off map ✉ St. John's Wood Road, NW8
☎ 020 7616 8500 Ⓔ St. John's Wood

MINISTRY OF SOUND

ministryofsound.com

Famed for its sound and lighting systems and known as the home of dance and house music, this legendary club—with its own record label—stars world-class DJs playing their own unique sets.

🚇 N8 ✉ 103 Gaunt Street, SE1 ☎ 020 7740 8600 Ⓣ Fri 10.30pm–6am, Sat 11pm–6am (last entry 2 hours before closing) Ⓔ Elephant and Castle

---

TICKET TIPS

Use the TKTS half-price ticket booth (in Leicester Square). Preview tickets and matinée tickets have reduced prices. Many theater box offices sell cheaper tickets from 10am on the day of performance. Go with friends and make a party booking at a reduced rate. Ask the National Theatre, Royal Court and other theaters about special discounts on particular performances; and keep student and senior citizen cards ready. Remember, the show is the same wherever you sit!

NATIONAL THEATRE

nationaltheatre.org.uk

Three performance spaces within the National Theatre complex—the Olivier Theatre, seating 1,100 people; the Lyttleton, seating 890; and the smaller Dorfman Theatre (400)—between them stage up to 30 productions a year. They range from re-imagined classics to modern masterpieces and new work by contemporary writers.

🚇 L6 ✉ South Bank, SE1 ☎ 020 7452 3000 information, tickets and tours
Ⓔ Embankment, Waterloo 🚆 Waterloo

O2 ACADEMY BRIXTON

o2academybrixton.co.uk

South London's favorite live music venue attracts big-name bands. It has an art deco interior and room for nearly 5,000 on the huge sloping dance floor. All the big rock bands have played and recorded here.

🚇 Off map ✉ 211 Stockwell Road, SW9
☎ 020 7771 3000 Ⓣ Times vary—check website for details Ⓔ Brixton, Stockwell

O2 ARENA

theo2.co.uk

A music and sports venue in the former Millennium Dome, the O2 Arena has a capacity of 20,000 and hosts big-name concerts, national awards ceremonies, tennis, basketball and darts championships.

🚇 Off map ✉ Peninsula Square, SE10
☎ 020 3784 7998 Ⓔ North Greenwich

OLD VIC

oldvictheatre.com

With a history dating back to 1818, this innovative old theater has had some famous artistic directors, including actor Kevin Spacey. It's run as a not-for-profit organization yet has staged many critically acclaimed productions, from family favorites to hard-hitting new drama. It's always worth checking out what's on.

➕ M7 ✉ The Cut, Waterloo Road, SE1
🚇 Waterloo, Southwark

THE PHEASANTRY, CHELSEA
pizzaexpresslive.com
There's live music every night at this engaging cabaret venue in a historic building that's now home to Pizza Express. The performers here know how to please their audiences.

➕ Off map ✉ 152 Kings Road, SW3
☎ 020 7439 4962 🕐 Show times vary
🚇 Sloane Square

PURCELL ROOM
southbankcentre.co.uk
Listen to chamber music, singers, musicians, poets and more in this intimate space.

➕ L6 ✉ South Bank, SE1 ☎ 020 7960
4200 🕐 Closed for renovation; due to re-open early 2018 🚇 Embankment, Waterloo

QUEEN ELIZABETH HALL
southbankcentre.co.uk
Come here for small orchestras, choirs, small-scale opera, piano recitals and dance.

➕ L6 ✉ South Bank, SE1 ☎ 020 7960
4200 🕐 Closed for renovation. Due to re-open early 2018 🚇 Embankment, Waterloo

THE RITZ
theritzlondon.com
To enter a bygone world, dress up for dinner and a dance on a Friday or Saturday at London's most opulent dining room (booking essential). For a more modest experience, go for afternoon tea in the Palm Court or the Rivoli Bar.

➕ G6 ✉ 150 Piccadilly, W1 ☎ 020 7493
8181 🚇 Green Park

ROUNDHOUSE
roundhouse.org.uk
This legendary venue has hosted some of the biggest names in rock and popular music, plus world-class music festivals, spoken word, dance, circus and cabaret acts and is recognized for launching the careers of emerging artists.

➕ Off map ✉ Chalk Farm Road, NW1
☎ 0300 678 9222 🕐 Show times vary
🚇 Chalk Farm

ROYAL ALBERT HALL
royalalberthall.com
Opened in 1871, this distinctive round building is best known for classical music and pop concerts, opera, ballet and the annual Henry Wood Promenade Concerts (Proms) held nightly from mid-July to mid-September. The 6,000-seat hall also hosts sporting events, and has smaller performance spaces.

➕ B7 ✉ Kensington Gore, SW7 ☎ 020
7589 8212 🚇 South Kensington

ENTERTAINMENT

ROYAL COURT/JERWOOD THEATRE UPSTAIRS

royalcourttheatre.com

The Royal Court has a lofty artistic reputation and presents only new work by leading or emerging playwrights. In the 1950s, John Osborne's *Look Back in Anger* shook up London theater forever, and today's productions follow in its wake.

➕ E9 ✉ Sloane Square, SW1 ☎ 020 7565 5000 🚇 Sloane Square

ROYAL FESTIVAL HALL

southbankcentre.co.uk

The Royal Festival Hall, at the heart of the Southbank Centre arts complex, stages world-class performances, with large-scale orchestral concerts, plus jazz and ballet.

➕ L6 ✉ South Bank, SE1 ☎ 020 7960 4200 🚇 Embankment, Waterloo

ROYAL OPERA HOUSE

roh.org.uk

The world's most acclaimed singers and dancers appear at the opulent Royal Opera House, home to the prestigious Royal Opera and Royal Ballet companies.

➕ K5 ✉ Bow Street, Covent Garden, WC2 ☎ 020 7304 4000 🚇 Covent Garden

SADLER'S WELLS THEATRE

sadlerswells.com

Sadler's Wells is one of the most electrifying dance theaters in Europe, with an exciting array of international and British companies presenting innovative dance of all genres.

➕ M1 ✉ Rosebery Avenue, EC1 ☎ 020 7863 8000 🚇 Angel

ST. JAMES'S, PICCADILLY

sjp.org.uk

This mid-17th-century church (▷ 73) by Sir Christopher Wren makes a sumptuous setting for lunchtime and evening choral and orchestral concerts.

➕ H6 ✉ 197 Piccadilly, W1 ☎ 020 7734 4511 🚇 Piccadilly Circus

ST. MARTIN-IN-THE-FIELDS

stmartin-in-the-fields.org

Baroque music is the focus of the free lunchtime concerts (Monday, Tuesday and Friday) and candlelit evening concerts (Thursday to Saturday) in this neo-classical church. There are also jazz nights in the crypt, where there's a café/restaurant.

➕ K5 ✉ Trafalgar Square, WC2 ☎ 020 7766 1100 🚇 Charing Cross

SALSA!

bar-salsa.com

Move to a Latin beat at this South American bar, restaurant and nightclub, where salsa dance classes are held every night and the menus feature tapas, fajitas, mojitos and caipirinhas.

➕ J4 ✉ 96 Charing Cross Road, WC2 ☎ 020 7379 3277 🕐 Sun–Thu 5pm–2am,

---

PUB MUSIC

This can be one of the least expensive and most enjoyable evenings out in London, and worth the trip to an offbeat location. For the price of a pint of beer (usually a huge choice) you can settle down to enjoy the ambience and listen to some of the best alternative music available in town—from folk, jazz and blues to rhythm and blues, soul and much more. Audiences tend to be friendly, loyal to their venue and happy to talk music.

Fri–Sat 5pm–3am. Open as a café Mon–Sat 10–5 🚇 Tottenham Court Road, Leicester Square

SHAKESPEARE'S GLOBE

shakespearesglobe.com
Plays by Shakespeare and his contemporaries are performed at this reconstruction of an open-air Elizabethan playhouse (▷ 48–49). The season runs from late April to the end of September. Tours run year-round.
✚ P6 ✉ 21 New Globe Walk, SE1 ☎ 020 7401 9919 🚇 London Bridge, Mansion House, Blackfriars, Southwark

THEATRE ROYAL, DRURY LANE

reallyusefultheatres.co.uk
The theater, built in 1812, stages mostly musicals. It is believed to be haunted—the most famous is the Man in Grey, said to walk around the Upper Circle.
✚ K5 ✉ Catherine Street, WC2 🚇 Covent Garden

WEMBLEY

wembleystadium.com
The state-of-the-art football stadium, where the English national team plays home games, also hosts a program of big-name pop and rock concerts.
✚ Off map ✉ Stadium Way, Wembley, Middlesex ☎ 0800 169 2007. Guided tours 0800 169 9933 🚇 Wembley Park 🚉 Wembley Stadium

WIGMORE HALL

wigmore-hall.org.uk
The hall was built in 1901 as a recital hall for Bechstein Pianos, so it has perfect acoustics. It is one of London's most beautiful settings for recitals and chamber music, especially for Sunday concerts.

Wembley Stadium

✚ F4 ✉ 36 Wigmore Street, W1 ☎ 020 7935 2141 🚇 Bond Street, Oxford Circus

WILTON'S MUSIC HALL

wiltons.org.uk
The world's oldest surviving Grand Music Hall may be hard to find (a door in the wall of a pedestrian alley), but it's worth it. An atmospheric arts and heritage venue that, like the East End around it, is experiencing revival after hard times, its diverse offering includes classical music, cabaret, opera, dance and magic.
✚ Off map ✉ 1 Graces Alley (off Ensign Street), E1 ☎ 020 7702 2789 🚇 Aldgate East, Tower Hill

YOUNG VIC

youngvic.org
One of London's most influential theaters, the Young Vic stages alternative productions of classics, new writing and experimental performances, often with famous actors taking lead roles.
✚ M7 ✉ 66 The Cut, SE1 ☎ 020 7922 2922 🚇 Waterloo, Southwark

Eat

There are places to eat across the city to suit all tastes and budgets. In this section establishments are listed alphabetically.

Introduction   **142**
Directory   **143**
Eating A–Z   **144**

EAT

Introduction

With more than 50 restaurants awarded one or more Michelin stars, the capital's reputation for fine dining continues to grow. Chefs have high profiles and London creates its own culinary trends. Using the finest-quality ingredients, modern British cuisine values simplicity and flavor, innovation and elegant presentation.

Cafés, Brasseries and Pubs

Multicultural London offers exciting restaurants serving a wide variety of different cuisines, ranging from European and cutting-edge contemporary to Indian, Asian and Middle Eastern. Tapas and sushi bars are popular and you don't have to look far to find a good spicy curry or fragrant Thai treat. No longer just an excuse to rest your feet, museum and art gallery cafés are as much of a destination as their exhibitions and, with their all-day menus, convivial brasseries have a relaxed Continental air. Gastropubs combine a fine setting with quality drinks and food.

Restaurant Chains

Try the Gourmet Burger Kitchen, Yo! Sushi, Wagamama, All-Bar-One and Masala Zone. Zizzi and Pizza Express are good pizza chains.

Afternoon Tea

A great British institution, afternoon tea is still available in hotels and tearooms from about 2 or 3pm. It always includes a pot of tea and something to eat, which can vary from dainty sandwiches and cakes to scones with clotted cream and jam.

DRESS CODE

In the past the British loved to dress for dinner, but these days only the most formal restaurants demand a jacket and tie. Customers should dress appropriately, however, to eat in upscale restaurants.

Top to bottom: The Palm Court at the Ritz; summertime alfresco dining in the capital; focaccia for sale at Borough Market; artisan breads, Borough Market

Directory

South Bank

British and Modern
Oxo Tower Bar,
  Brasserie &
  Restaurant
Roast
European
Baltic
Gastropubs/Bars
Anchor Bankside
Anchor & Hope
Lighter Bites
Tate Modern Café

Fleet Street to the Tower

Asian
Banh Mi Bay
British and Modern
The Café Below
St. John
European
Club Gascon
Famous Chefs
Fifteen
Gastropubs/Bars
The Peasant
Lighter Bites
Wren's Pantry
Vegetarian
Vanilla Black

Covent Garden to Regent's Park

Asian
Benares
Chaopraya Eat-Thai
Masala Zone
Rasa W1
Brasseries/Brunch
Christopher's
Joe Allen
British and Modern
Rules

European
Gaby's Deli
Icebar London
Olivelli
Villandry
Wild Honey
Famous Chefs
The Square
Tom's Kitchen
Gastropubs/Bars
The Dog and Duck
Lowlander Grand
  Café
International
Ceviche
Vegetarian
Wild Food Café

Westminster and St. James's

Asian
Tamarind
British and Modern
Portrait Restaurant
The Wolseley
Lighter Bites
Inn the Park

Around Hyde Park

Asian
Amaya
Royal China
British and Modern
Babylon
Bibendum
Maggie Jones's
Famous Chefs
Le Gavroche
Lighter Bites
The Orangery

Farther Afield

British and Modern
The Glasshouse

Grainstore
Medlar
European
Ottolenghi
La Poule au Pot
Providores & Tapa
  Room
Gastropubs/Bars
The Gun

EAT

Eating A–Z

AMAYA £££

amaya.biz

With a string of positive reviews and a Michelin star to its name, Amaya offers sophisticated Indian grills, exquisitely presented, in a vibrant and upscale Knightsbridge setting complete with a theatrical show kitchen.

➕ E8 ✉ Halkin Arcade, Motcomb Street, SW1 ☎ 020 7823 1166 ⏰ Mon–Sat 12.30–2.15, 6.30–11.30, Sun 12.45–2.45, 6.30–10.15 🚇 Knightsbridge

ANCHOR BANKSIDE £

taylor-walker.co.uk

This historic pub with its maze of tiny rooms and pleasant garden terrace enjoys excellent river views.

RIVERSIDE EATING

London is exploiting the potential of its riverside views. As well as traditional pubs such as Anchor Bankside (▷ above) many new restaurants are opening along the South Bank. The most spectacular views are from the Oxo Tower Restaurant (▷ 149) and Tate Modern's rooftop restaurant at Bankside (▷ 151). There are lower but still impressive views from the eateries that line the Thames in the Southbank Centre (▷ 83). The Mayflower, London's oldest Thameside pub (✉ 117 Rotherhithe Street, SE16), is on the original mooring point of the Pilgrim Fathers' ship.

Food is traditional British, with fish and chips and Sunday roasts.

➕ P6 ✉ Bankside, 34 Park Street, SE1 ☎ 020 7407 1577 ⏰ Restaurant: Mon–Sat 12–10, Sun 12–9 🚇 London Bridge

ANCHOR & HOPE ££

anchorandhopepub.co.uk

A quality gastropub serving good British food. There are no reservations (except for Sunday lunch) so arrive early or be prepared to wait.

➕ M7 ✉ 36 The Cut, SE1 ☎ 020 7928 9898 ⏰ Tue–Sat 11–11, Mon 5–11, Sun 12.30–3.15. Dining room opens at 12 for lunch and 6 for dinner; names are taken for first sitting from 5.15 🚇 Southwark, Waterloo

BABYLON ££–£££

virginlimitededition.com

Take a seat in the rooftop gardens, complete with oak trees, flamingos and expansive views over London, for elegant modern British cuisine.

➕ Off map ✉ The Roof Garden, 99 Kensington High Street, W8 ☎ 020 7368 3993 ⏰ Mon–Sat 12–12, Sun 12–7 🚇 High Street Kensington

BALTIC £–££

balticrestaurant.co.uk

Head to the bar for some serious cocktails, then on to the dramatic contemporary restaurant for modern Polish and Eastern European food and jazz every Sunday from 7pm.

➕ N7 ✉ 74 Blackfriars Road, SE1 ☎ 020 7928 1111 ⏰ Restaurant: Mon–Sat 5.30–11.15, Tue–Sat lunch 12–3, Sun 12–4.30, 5.30–10.30. Bar: 12–12 🚇 Southwark

BANH MI BAY £

banhmibay.co.uk

This bright and light Vietnamese diner in a country-kitchen style is

popular with local workers at lunchtime (it does takeouts, too).
🔼 L3 ✉ 4–6 Theobalds Road, Holborn, WC1 ☎ 020 7831 4079 🕐 Mon–Fri 11.30–4, 5.30–9.45, Sat 12–9.45 🚇 Chancery Lane

BENARES £££
benaresrestaurant.com
Atul Kochhar serves subtly spiced and stylish Indian dishes in his Michelin-starred restaurant. There are innovative vegetarian options.
➕ G5 ✉ 12a Berkeley Square House, Berkeley Square, W1 ☎ 020 7629 8886 🕐 Mon–Fri 12–2.30, 5.30–10.45, Sat 12–3, 5.30–10.45, Sun 6–9.45 🚇 Green Park

BIBENDUM ££–£££
bibendum.co.uk
In a landmark building with art-nouveau elegance and charm, enjoy classic French food with British flair in the restaurant or go for relaxed luxury in the Oyster Bar.
➕ D9 ✉ 81 Fulham Road, SW3 ☎ 020 7581 5817; Oyster Bar 020 7590 1186 🕐 Mon–Fri 12–2.30, 7–11, Sat–Sun 12.30–3, 7–10.30 (Sat 11); Oyster Bar Mon–Sat 11.30–10, Sun 12–10 🚇 South Kensington

THE CAFÉ BELOW £
cafebelow.co.uk
In the medieval crypt of a Wren church with walls dating back to before 1066, you'll find fresh seasonal ingredients on British-,

French- and Mediterranean-influenced menus.
➕ P4 ✉ St. Mary-le-Bow, Cheapside, FC? ☎ 020 7329 0789 🕐 Mon–Fri 7.30–2.30 🚇 Bank, St. Paul's, Mansion House

CEVICHE £–££
cevicheuk.com
Peruvian food is the big new taste sensation and Ceviche is the hot London source of this tasty and healthy cuisine.
➕ J4 ✉ 17 Frith Street, W1 ☎ 020 7292 2040 🕐 Mon–Sat 12–11.30, Sun 12–10.15 🚇 Tottenham Court Road, Leicester Square, Piccadilly Circus

CHAOPRAYA EAT-THAI ££
eatthai.net
Enjoy classic Thai dishes at this quiet, stylish restaurant located just behind Oxford Street.
➕ F4 ✉ 22 St. Christopher's Place, W1 ☎ 020 7486 0777 🕐 Daily 12–3, 6–11 🚇 Bond Street

CHRISTOPHER'S ££
christophersgrill.com
One of the best places in London for a genuine American brunch, Christopher's is in a beautiful Victorian town house with a Martini Bar on the ground floor.
➕ K5 ✉ 18 Wellington Street, WC2 ☎ 020 7240 4222 🕐 Mon–Wed 11.30am–midnight, Thu–Sat 11.30am–1.30am, Sun 11.30–10.30 🚇 Covent Garden

EAT

CLUB GASCON £££

clubgascon.com

Good for that special dinner, Michelin-starred Club Gascon serves unusual, robust dishes from the southwest of France. Reserve well in advance.

➕ N3 ✉ 57 West Smithfield, EC1 ☎ 020 7600 6144 🕐 Tue–Thu 12–2, 6–9.30, Fri 12–2, 6–10, Sat 6–10 🚇 Barbican, Farringdon

THE DOG AND DUCK £

nicholsonspubs.co.uk/
thedoganddducksoholondon

Quality beers, cask ales and hearty classic British pub food feature in this historic Soho pub that's full of character and boasts of serving John Constable, George Orwell and Madonna.

➕ J4 ✉ 18 Bateman Street, W1 ☎ 020 7494 0697 🕐 Mon–Thu 11–11, Fri–Sat 11am–11.30pm, Sun 12–10.30 🚇 Tottenham Court Road

FIFTEEN ££

fifteen.net

Jamie Oliver takes inspiration from around the world for his rustic yet elegant dishes. The cocktail bar has tempting snacks.

➕ Q1 ✉ 15 Westland Place, N1 ☎ 020 3375 1515 🕐 Mon–Thu 12–3, 6–10.30, Fri–Sat 12–3, 5.30–10.30, Sun 12–3, 6–9.30 🚇 Old Street

GABY'S DELI £

Inspired by a New York Jewish diner, this is the place to head for Mediterranean and Mideastern staples—the falafels are legendary—either to eat in or take out.

➕ J5 ✉ 30 Charing Cross Road, WC2 ☎ 020 7836 4233 🕐 Mon–Sat 10am–11pm 🚇 Leicester Square

LE GAVROCHE £££

le-gavroche.co.uk

Michel Roux's two Michelin-starred restaurant fuses amazing food,

A classic club sandwich

Modern British cuisine uses the finest ingredients

wine and service into an unforget-
table experience. Reservations are
taken three months in advance.
➕ E5 ✉ 43 Upper Brook Street, W1
☎ 020 7408 0881 🕐 Tue–Fri 12–2, 6–10,
Sat 6–10 🚇 Marble Arch

THE GLASSHOUSE £££
glasshouserestaurant.co.uk
The Glasshouse serves notable
modern dishes, beautifully pre-
sented. The wine list is impressive.
Reserve in advance.
➕ Off map ✉ 14 Station Parade, Kew,
TW9 ☎ 020 8940 6777 🕐 Mon–Sat
12–2.30, 6.30–10.30, Sun 12.30–3, 7–9.30
🚇 Kew Gardens

GRAINSTORE ££
grainstore.com
Chef Bruno Loubet's imaginative
and eclectic menus feature fresh
and seasonal ingredients and it's
the vegetables that star in this
award-winning restaurant in the
King's Cross quarter.
➕ Off map ✉ Granary Square,
1–3 Stable Street, N1 ☎ 020 7324 4466
🕐 Mon–Wed 10am–11.30pm, Thu–Sat
10am–midnight, Sun 10.30–3.30
🚇 Green Park

THE GUN £–££
thegundocklands.com
A popular gastropub on Canary
Wharf, with a long history and
stunning views, The Gun serves
imaginative, seasonal British food.
Seafood and grills feature on the
restaurant menu, while the pub
menu, served in the bar area and
on the terrace, focuses on updated
British classics like pie and mash,
fish and chips and burgers.
➕ Off map ✉ 27 Coldharbour, Isle of
Dogs, E14 ☎ 020 7515 5222 🕐 Daily
11.30–midnight 🚇 Canary Wharf, Blackwall

ICEBAR LONDON £–££
icebarlondon.com
Sip a cocktail in London's "coolest"
bar, created from Swedish ice.
Entry is by timed ticket and ses-
sions last 40 minutes. Capes and
mittens are provided. There's a
warm bar, too, and a restaurant
serving hearty food.
➕ H5 ✉ 31–33 Heddon Street, W1
☎ 020 7478 8910 🕐 Opening times vary,
call or check website 🚇 Oxford Circus,
Piccadilly Circus

INN THE PARK £
peytonandbyrne.co.uk/inn-the-park
Enjoy inspired British food with
lake and park views. Afternoon tea
is served daily 3–4.30pm.
➕ J7 ✉ St. James's Park, SW1 ☎ 020
7451 9999 🕐 Mon–Fri 8am–9pm, Sat 9–9,
Sun 9–4.30 🚇 St. James's Park

JOE ALLEN ££
joeallen.co.uk
For American food and beer head
to this dependably convivial and
clublike establishment.
Reservations are essential.
➕ K5 ✉ 13 Exeter Street, WC2
☎ 020 7836 0651 🕐 Mon–Fri 12–12 (Fri
till 1am), Sat 10am–1am, Sun 11–10.30
🚇 Covent Garden

EAT

THE BILL
When the bill arrives, read it carefully.
A 12.5 percent service charge, or more,
may have been added. If the service you
received has not been satisfactory, or if
you prefer to tip your waiter in cash, ask
them to remove it. A hefty bill can quickly
mount up so, to avoid any unpleasant
surprises, check whether VAT and coffee
are included and if there's a cover charge.
Order tap water if you don't want to pay
for bottled water.

The unmistakable OXO Tower

LOWLANDER GRAND CAFÉ £

lowlander.com

This Belgian bar and brasserie is in a great spot for a pretheater meal. Try the rib-eye *steak frites*.

➕ K4 ✉ 36 Drury Lane, WC2 ☎ 020 7379 7446 🕑 Mon–Wed 10–10, Thu 10am–11pm, Fri–Sat 9am–midnight, Sun 9am–10.30pm 🚇 Covent Garden

MAGGIE JONES'S ££

maggie-jones.co.uk

This cozy Kensington institution is much loved for its informality, excellent wine list and traditional, classic British food.

➕ Off map ✉ 6 Old Court Place, Kensington Church Street, W8 ☎ 020 7937 6462 🕑 Daily 12–2.30, 6–11 (Sun till 10) 🚇 High Street Kensington

MASALA ZONE ££

masalazone.com

From the creators of Chutney Mary and Veeraswamy, both known for their authentic dishes, comes an informal setting for *thalis* and Indian street food. There are other branches in the capital.

➕ H5 ✉ 9 Marshall Street, W1 ☎ 020 7287 9966 🕑 Mon–Fri 12–11, Sat 12.30–11, Sun 12.30–10.30 🚇 Oxford Circus

MEDLAR ££

medlarrestaurant.co.uk

Offering imaginative dishes using fresh seasonal ingredients and with wines chosen by a master sommelier, Medlar is consistently praised for taste, presentation, good service and the excellent value of its set-price menu.

➕ Off map ✉ 438 King's Road, SW10 ☎ 020 7349 1400 🕑 Mon–Sat 12–3, 6.30–10.30, Sun 12–3, 6–9.30 🚇 Sloane Square, Fulham Broadway

OLIVELLI £–££

ristoranteolivelli.co.uk

The flagship venue of London's intimate, family-owned, Sicilian restaurants, Olivelli is minutes from Tottenham Court Road and Oxford Street. The regional menu includes award-winning homemade pizza, pasta, salads, meat and fish dishes and delicious desserts.

➕ J3 ✉ 35 Store Street, WC1 ☎ 020 7255 2554 🕑 Mon–Sat 11.30–11, Sun 12–10 🚇 Goodge Street

THE ORANGERY £

orangerykensingtonpalace.co.uk

A fine 18th-century building overlooking Kensington Palace's beautiful formal gardens creates

---

SET-PRICE MENUS

Many of London's pricier restaurants offer less expensive set-price menus at lunchtime. Try the three-course Michelin-starred lunch of Hélène Darroze at the Connaught Hotel (➕ E5 ✉ 16 Carlos Place, W1 ☎ 020 3147 7200) or the lunch menu at Medlar (▷ above).

the perfect setting for elegant light lunches or afternoon tea—cucumber sandwiches and scones with jam and cream.

⊞ A6 ⊠ Kensington Palace, Kensington Gardens, W8 ☎ 020 3166 6113
🌐 Mar–Oct daily 10–6; Nov–Feb daily 10–4
🚇 High Street Kensington

OTTOLENGHI £

ottolenghi.co.uk

Merely looking at the restaurant is sustaining; eating here around the communal tables is even better. The Mediterranean-influenced dishes are fresh, colorful and full of flavor. Favorites include roast chicken with chilli and basil and roasted sweet potato with pecan and maple syrup. The restaurant is opposite the Almeida Theatre.

⊞ Off map ⊠ 287 Upper Street, N1
☎ 020 7288 1454 🌐 Mon–Sat 8am–10.30pm, Sun 9am–7pm 🚇 Angel, Highbury & Islington

OXO TOWER BAR, BRASSERIE AND RESTAURANT ££–£££

harveynichols.com

Look out over London while feasting on vibrantly modern British and pan-Asian food. There are plenty of outdoor tables but reservations are essential.

⊞ M6 ⊠ 8th Floor, Oxo Tower Wharf, Barge House Street, SE1 ☎ 020 7803 3888
🌐 Opening times vary, call or check website
🚇 Blackfriars

THE PEASANT £–££

thepeasant.co.uk

Expect a warm welcome at this north London gastropub. Classic and modern British food is served in the bar, with more sophisticated flavors from the à la carte menu on offer in the upstairs restaurant.

⊞ N2 ⊠ 240 St. John Street, EC1 ☎ 020 7336 7726 🌐 Mon–Sat 12–11, Sun 12–10.30 🚇 Farringdon

PORTRAIT RESTAURANT ££

npg.org.uk

Up on level three of the National Portrait Gallery, every table here has a fine view over London. Try the salmon with cream sauce for a summer lunch. Reservations are essential.

⊞ J5 ⊠ National Portrait Gallery, St. Martin's Place, WC2 ☎ 020 7312 2490
🌐 Thu–Sat 10–10, Sun–Wed 10–5
🚇 Leicester Square, Charing Cross

LA POULE AU POT ££

pouleaupot.co.uk

A Belgravia institution, loved as much for its romantic, retro country atmosphere as its classic French cooking. Think bouillabaisse, boeuf bourguignon, cassoulet and tarte tatin. In summer, the outdoor terrace is popular for alfresco trysts.

⊞ Off map ⊠ 231 Ebury Street, SW1
☎ 020 7730 7763 🌐 Mon–Sat 12–11, Sun 12–10 🚇 Sloane Square

EAT

PROVIDORES & TAPA ROOM ££

theprovidores.co.uk

Enjoy inventive fusion cooking and New Zealand wines at this café, wine bar and fine-dining restaurant. The weekend brunches are highly recommended.

⊞ F3 ✉ 109 Marylebone High Street, W1 ☎ 020 7935 6175 🕓 Mon–Fri 8am–10.30pm, Sat 9am–10.30pm, Sun 9am–10pm 🚇 Baker Street

RASA W1 £

rasarestaurants.com

One of several Rasa restaurants in the capital, Rasa W1 serves inspired cooking from Kerala in southwest India, with seafood and vegetarian dishes as specialties.

⊞ G4 ✉ 6 Dering Street, W1 ☎ 020 7629 1346 🕓 Mon–Sat 12–3, 6–11, Sun 1–3, 6–9 🚇 Oxford Circus, Bond Street

ROAST ££–£££

roast-restaurant.com

Fine modern British food is served at this restaurant in Borough Market. Many of the seasonal ingredients come from the market stalls. While you eat, you can enjoy the view over the market or out toward The Shard and St. Paul's. Sunday lunch is a set menu only.

⊞ Q6 ✉ The Floral Hall, Stoney Street, SE1 ☎ 020 3006 6111 🕓 Mon–Fri 7–10.45, 12–3.45, 5.30–10.45, Sat 8.30–11.30, 12–3.45, 6–10.45, Sun 11.30–6.30 🚇 London Bridge

ROYAL CHINA £–££

theroyalchina.co.uk

Reserve a table or join the long lines for the best dim sum in town, served between 12 and 4.45.

⊞ A5 ✉ 13 Queensway, W2 ☎ 020 7221 2535 🕓 Mon–Sat 12–11, Sun 11–10 🚇 Queensway

RULES ££

rules.co.uk

Rules, founded in 1798 and claiming to be London's oldest restaurant, serves traditional English dishes, such as oysters, game and pies, in plush Edwardian rooms.

⊞ K5 ✉ 35 Maiden Lane, WC2 ☎ 020 7836 5314 🕓 Daily 12–12 🚇 Covent Garden

ST. JOHN ££

stjohngroup.uk.com

The robust dishes on offer range from rabbit to oxtail to serious puddings, such as lemon posset.

⊞ N3 ✉ 26 St. John Street, EC1 ☎ 020 7521 0848 🕓 Mon–Fri 12–3, 6–11, Sat 6pm–11pm, Sun 12.30–4 🚇 Farringdon

THE SQUARE £££

squarerestaurant.com

Impressive modern French cuisine from two Michelin-starred chef Philip Howard is matched by a chic but formal Mayfair interior.

⊞ G5 ✉ 6–10 Bruton Street, W1 ☎ 020 7495 7100 🕓 Mon–Fri 12–2.30, 6.30–10, Sat 12–2.30, 6–10.30, Sun 6.30–9.30 🚇 Bond Street, Green Park

TAMARIND ££

tamarindrestaurant.com

Contemporary Indian cuisine is impeccably presented in a Mayfair restaurant with a long-held Michelin star. The lunch menu is especially good value.

✚ G6 ✉ 20 Queen Street, W1 ☎ 020 7629 3561 ⏰ Mon–Sat 12–2.45, 5.30–10.45, Sun 12–2.45, 6–10.15 Ⓜ Green Park

TATE MODERN CAFÉ £

tate.org.uk

Take a break from the art to enjoy upscale café food and Thames views on Level 1 of Tate Modern. For a grander meal, book at the rooftop restaurant.

✚ N6 ✉ Tate Modern, Bankside, SE1 ☎ 020 7401 5104 ⏰ Daily 10–6 Ⓜ Blackfriars, Southwark

TOM'S KITCHEN £–££

tomskitchen.co.uk

This is a vibrant, modern British restaurant, deli and summer terrace bar set in the splendor of Somerset House (▷ 50–51).

✚ L5 ✉ Somerset House, Strand, WC2 ☎ 020 7845 4646 ⏰ Lunch Mon–Fri 12–3; dinner Mon–Sat 6–10; brunch Sat–Sun 10–4; deli Mon–Fri 8–6, Sat–Sun 10–6 Ⓜ Blackfriars

VANILLA BLACK £–££

vanillablack.co.uk

Vanilla Black has a reputation as one of the finest vegetarian restaurants in London, using original flavor combinations created with modern culinary techniques.

✚ M4 ✉ 17–18 Took's Court, EC4 ☎ 020 7242 2622 ⏰ Mon–Sat 12–2.30, 6–10 Ⓜ Chancery Lane

VILLANDRY ££

villandry.com

Villandry offers an array of dining spaces. The emphasis is on light Mediterranean fare and steaks.

✚ G3 ✉ 170 Great Portland Street, W1 ☎ 020 7631 3131 ⏰ Mon–Fri 7.30am–10.30pm, Sat 8am–10.30pm, Sun 9–6 Ⓜ Great Portland Street, Regent's Park

WILD FOOD CAFÉ £

wildfoodcafe.com

This café in Covent Garden is dedicated to making you feel great, with a host of innovative raw and plant-based dishes (wholefood, vegan and vegetarian).

✚ K4 ✉ 1st floor, 14 Neal's Yard, WC2 ☎ 020 7419 2014 ⏰ Tue–Thu 11.30–9, Fri–Sat 11.30–10, Sun 11.30–7 Ⓜ Covent Garden

WILD HONEY ££–£££

wildhoneyrestaurant.co.uk

Enjoy quality modern European cooking in a stylishly simple Mayfair setting. The set lunch and pretheater menus are good value.

✚ G5 ✉ 12 St. George Street, W1 ☎ 020 7758 9160 ⏰ Mon–Sat 12–2.30, 6–10.30 Ⓜ Oxford Circus, Bond Street

THE WOLSELEY ££

thewolseley.com

The Grand Café tradition continues at the Wolseley in Piccadilly. Start the day in art deco grandeur, or relax over afternoon tea after visiting the Royal Academy.

✚ H6 ✉ 160 Piccadilly, W1 ☎ 020 7499 6996 ⏰ Mon–Fri 7am–midnight, Sat 8am–midnight, Sun 8am–11pm Ⓜ Green Park, Piccadilly Circus

WREN'S PANTRY £–££

searcysstpauls.co.uk

In the crypt beneath Wren's great St. Paul's Cathedral (▷ 44–45), a quiet retreat from the crowds above, the coffeehouse offers good-value soup, sandwiches, homemade cakes and hot meals. Traditional afternoon tea is served in the adjacent Wren's Tea Room.

✚ N4 ✉ St. Paul's Churchyard, off Paternoster Row, EC4 ☎ 020 7248 1574 ⏰ Daily 9–5 Ⓜ St. Paul's

Sleep

With options ranging from the luxurious to simple budget hotels, London has accommodations to suit everyone. In this section establishments are listed alphabetically.

Introduction	**154**
Directory	**155**
Sleeping A–Z	**155**

SLEEP

Introduction

London has many excellent hotels but room rates are very high, and it is certainly worth searching for special offers. You will find weekend and winter rates are often less expensive.

Reservations

Many hotels will ask you to prepay your reservation, or confirm with a credit card, and will charge a fee if you cancel at short notice or fail to turn up. Most hotels have rooms of different sizes, so always ask if there is a choice. Small hotels and guesthouses in historic buildings may not have a lift (elevator).

Outside Central London

If you are prepared to take a slightly longer bus or Tube ride to reach the sights, staying in a residential suburb provides a less expensive alternative to a pricey city-center hotel.

Budget Accommodations

Consider alternatives to hotels, such as renting an apartment, staying in a bed-and-breakfast (B&B) or staying with a London family (for online information visit bedandbreakfast. com, athomeinlondon.co.uk or the tourist board's visitlondon.com). During student vacations, inexpensive accommodations are offered by London university halls of residence (see universityrooms.co.uk and ish.org.uk). Youth hostels are another inexpensive option (yha.org.uk).

NOISE LEVELS

As most of London's accommodation options are situated on busy streets, noise can be a problem. Some hotels have double glazing, but that can make rooms unbearably stuffy, especially since air-conditioning is not standard. If you value peace and quiet, look for hotels on side streets in residential areas or request a room at the rear or higher up in the building.

Top to bottom: The exclusive Claridge's Hotel; the grand entrance to The Dorchester; London's top hotels offer superb service; a room at the Grosvenor Hotel

Directory

South Bank

Budget
Tune Hotel Westminster

Fleet Street to the Tower

Mid-Range
Chamberlain
Zetter Rooms
Luxury
Andaz
Malmaison
The Rookery

Covent Garden to Regent's Park

Budget
Morgan
Mid-Range
Academy
Luxury
Charlotte Street Hotel
Covent Garden Hotel
Hazlitt's
Savoy

Westminster and St. James's

Luxury
The Goring
The Ritz

Around Hyde Park

Budget
Easyhotel
Kensington House
Pavilion Hotel
Mid-Range
22 York Street
Aster House
The Leonard
My Chelsea
Luxury
The Berkeley
Blakes
The Dorchester
The Halkin

Farther Afield

Mid-Range
The Beaver
Henley House
Portobello

Sleeping A–Z

PRICES

Prices are approximate and based on a double room for one night.

£££	Over £250
£££	£150–£250
£	under £150

22 YORK STREET ££

22yorkstreet.co.uk
This elegant five-story Georgian town house close to Regent's Park has been transformed into a quality bed-and-breakfast.

➕ E3 ✉ 22 York Street, W1 ☎ 020 7224 2990 🚇 Baker Street

ACADEMY ££

theacademyhotel.co.uk
Conveniently located for the British Museum, this elegant 49-room boutique hotel is set in five restored Georgian town houses. It has a cozy bar and offers a traditional afternoon tea, complete with crustless sandwiches and scones with jam.

➕ J3 ✉ 21 Gower Street, WC1 ☎ 020 7631 4115 🚇 Goodge Street

ANDAZ £££

londonliverpoolstreet.andaz.hyatt.com
Casual 21st-century luxury is the theme of this stylishly converted Victorian railway hotel with a Japanese restaurant, brasserie, English pub and wine lounge.
✚ R3 ✉ 40 Liverpool Street, EC2 ☎ 020 7961 1234 🚇 Liverpool Street

ASTER HOUSE ££

asterhouse.com
Aster House stands with other chic B&Bs in a smart South Kensington stuccoed terrace, near the museums. You can enjoy the garden and palm-filled conservatory.
✚ C9 ✉ 3 Sumner Place, SW7 ☎ 020 7581 5888 🚇 South Kensington

THE BEAVER £

beaverhotel.co.uk
The Beaver offers B&B accommodation on a tree-lined Victorian crescent in Earl's Court, near South Kensington's museums.
✚ Off map ✉ 57–59 Philbeach Gardens, SW5 ☎ 020 7373 4553 🚇 Earl's Court

THE BERKELEY £££

the-berkeley.co.uk
Guests at this luxury Knightsbridge hotel enjoy traditional elegance,

LOCATION

It is well worth perusing the London map to decide where you are likely to spend most of your time. Then select a hotel in that area or accessible to it by Underground on a direct line, so you avoid having to change trains. London is vast and it takes time to cross, particularly by bus and costly taxis. By paying a little more to be in the heart of the city, you will save on travel time and costs.

plus famed service and food. Facilities include a spa, rooftop pool and two great restaurants.
✚ E7 ✉ Wilton Place, SW1 ☎ 020 7235 6000 🚇 Hyde Park Corner, Knightsbridge

BLAKES £££

blakeshotels.com
Designer Anoushka Hempel has achieved sumptuous decadence in this South Kensington boutique hotel with a celebrity guest list. There's a stunning restaurant, a stylish bar and a tranquil courtyard.
✚ Off map ✉ 33 Roland Gardens, SW7 ☎ 020 7370 6701 🚇 South Kensington, Gloucester Road

CHAMBERLAIN £–££

thechamberlainhotel.co.uk
In lavishly converted 20th-century offices in the City of London, this hotel has 64 comfortable bedrooms, some with their own outdoor roof terrace. There is a popular pub on the premises.
✚ S5 ✉ 130–135 Minories, EC3 ☎ 020 7680 1500 🚇 Aldgate, Tower Hill

CHARLOTTE STREET HOTEL £££

firmdalehotels.com
Close to London's theater district, Kit and Tim Kemp's boutique cocktail of comfort and fairy-tale Englishness spans individually designed rooms and suites and a restaurant with a Bloomsbury Group theme.
✚ H3 ✉ 15 Charlotte Street, W1 ☎ 020 7806 2000 🚇 Goodge Street

COVENT GARDEN HOTEL £££

firmdalehotels.com
Another of Kit Kemp's stylish boutiqe hotels, the hotel's location and deluxe rooms and suites attract film stars who also

appreciate the wood-paneled drawing room and library.

➕ J4 ✉ 10 Monmouth Street, WC2 ☎ 020 7806 1000 Ⓔ Leicester Square

THE DORCHESTER £££

dorchestercollection.com

The Dorchester is one of London's finest hotels. Deliciously art deco, it is a London landmark from its grand entrance and piano bar to the Oliver Messel suite, from the luxurious spa to the famous Grill. It boasts the only UK hotel restaurant with three Michelin stars.

➕ F6 ✉ Park Lane, W1 ☎ 020 7629 8888 Ⓔ Green Park, Hyde Park Corner

EASYHOTEL £

easyhotel.com

EasyHotel is inexpensive and very basic. The rooms are tiny, many without a window, but all come with their own compact shower room. There is no provision for meals on site, and you pay extra for television and internet access.

➕ A8 ✉ 14 Lexham Gardens, W8 ⌨ Reserve by website only Ⓔ Earl's Court, Gloucester Road; other locations available

THE GORING £££

thegoring.com

High standards of old-fashioned hospitality and service make this splendid hotel memorable. It's where the Middleton family stayed before Kate's wedding to Prince William.

➕ G8 ✉ Beeston Place, Grosvenor Gardens, SW1 ☎ 020 7396 9000 Ⓔ Victoria

THE HALKIN £££

comohotels.com/thehalkin

With a stylish blend of Western and Asian aesthetics, the contemporary design of this luxury

The Dorchester, one of the capital's finest hotels

MODERN HOTELS

London has many contemporary hotels, from starkly minimal to sumptuously luxurious. At the top end, try the Andaz Hotel (▷ 156), One Aldwych (✉ 1 Aldwych, WC2 ☎ 020 7300 1000, onealdwych.com), Kit Kemp's eight London hotels (firmdalehotels.com), Sanderson (✉ 50 Berners Street, W1 ☎ 020 7300 1400, sandersonlondon.com), No. 5 Maddox Street (✉ 5 Maddox Street, W1 ☎ 020 7647 0200, living-rooms.co.uk) or St. Martin's Lane (✉ 45 St. Martin's Lane, WC2 ☎ 020 7300 5500, stmartinslane.com).

The Savoy, a byword for luxury

boutique hotel extends to its spa and Michelin-starred Spanish restaurant.

➕ F7 ✉ 4 Halkin Street, SW1 ☎ 020 7333 1000 🚇 Hyde Park Corner

HAZLITT'S £££

hazlittshotel.com

The 23-room Hazlitt's has near-perfect period decoration in three 18th-century houses, plus it's in a superb location for Theatreland.

➕ J4 ✉ 6 Frith Street, W1 ☎ 020 7434 1771 🚇 Tottenham Court Road

HENLEY HOUSE £–££

henleyhousehotel.com

In this boutique hotel the decor is light and modern, the facilities are good and breakfast is served in the garden conservatory.

➕ Off map ✉ 30 Barkston Gardens, SW5 ☎ 020 7370 4111 🚇 Earl's Court

KENSINGTON HOUSE £–££

kenhouse.com

This beautifully restored 19th-century property provides

contemporary accommodations in the heart of Kensington. The 41 bedrooms are light and stylish.

➕ A7 ✉ 15–16 Prince of Wales Terrace, W8 ☎ 020 7937 2345 🚇 High Street Kensington

THE LEONARD ££–£££

theleonard.com

A discreet, small hotel, the Leonard personifies traditional classic elegance. The spacious rooms, suites and family rooms are comfortable and there's a good restaurant.

➕ E4 ✉ 15 Seymour Street, W1 ☎ 020 7935 2010 🚇 Marble Arch

MALMAISON ££–£££

malmaison.com

In Malmaison's signature edgy decor, the rooms in this cleverly converted former nurses' home are stylishly contemporary—all stripped wood floors, exposed brick walls and moody lighting—as is the Chez Mal brasserie.

➕ N3 ✉ 18 Charterhouse Square, EC1 ☎ 020 3750 9402 🚇 Farringdon

MORGAN £

morganhotel.co.uk

Reserve well ahead for this small, friendly and well-located family-run hotel set over two Georgian buildings near the British Museum.

➕ J3 ✉ 24 Bloomsbury Street, WC1 ☎ 020 7636 3735 🚇 Tottenham Court Road, Russell Square

SLEEP

MY CHELSEA ££

myhotels.com/chelsea

The cool, clean lines of urban chic and a relaxed color scheme distinguish this small hotel, where My Kitchen offers healthy meals.

➕ D9 ✉ 35 Ixworth Place, SW3
☎ 020 7225 7500 🚇 South Kensington, Sloane Square

PAVILION HOTEL £

pavilionhoteluk.com

Behind a plain facade lie 30 eccentric, brightly colored themed rooms in a hotel that describes itself as "fashion rock 'n' roll."

➕ C4 ✉ 34–36 Sussex Gardens, W2
☎ 020 7262 0905 🚇 Paddington

PORTOBELLO ££–£££

portobello-hotel.co.uk

In this romantic Notting Hill retreat, each charming room has a distinct personality and the elegant Sitting Room enjoys views over the private gardens.

➕ Off map ✉ 22 Stanley Gardens, W11
☎ 020 7727 2777 🚇 Notting Hill Gate

THE RITZ £££

theritzlondon.com

Guests enjoy sumptuous luxury, with traditional style, gilt decor and the great first-floor promenade to London's most beautiful dining room, overlooking Green Park.

➕ G6 ✉ 150 Piccadilly, W1 ☎ 020 7493 8181 🚇 Green Park

THE ROOKERY £££

rookeryhotel.com

Full of period charm with wood paneling, open fires and antique furniture, there's a club-like atmosphere in this boutique hotel.

➕ N3 ✉ 12 Peter's Lane, Cowcross Street, EC1 ☎ 020 7336 0931 🚇 Farringdon

SAVOY £££

fairmont.com/savoy-london

A top-to-toe refurbishment has brought this grand London hotel firmly into the 21st century while preserving the grand Edwardian decor. It has a perfect spot next to the Thames, just a stone's throw from Covent Garden.

➕ L5 ✉ Strand, WC2 ☎ 020 7836 4343
🚇 Covent Garden

TUNE HOTEL WESTMINSTER £

tunehotels.com

The rooms are tiny, some without even a window, and very basic, but the beds are comfortable and rooms all have bathrooms with power showers.

➕ M8 ✉ 118–120 Westminster Bridge Road, SE1 ☎ 020 7633 9317
🚇 Lambeth North

ZETTER ROOMS ££–£££

thezetter.com

In a clever repurposing of a Victorian warehouse, the rooms have mood lighting and workstations, raindance showers and duck down pillows

➕ N2 ✉ St. John's Square, 86–88 Clerkenwell Road, EC1 ☎ 020 7324 4444
🚇 Farringdon

BARGAIN LUXURY

To be pampered amid sumptuous surroundings may be an essential part of your trip. London's most luxurious hotels have been built with no expense spared. Hotel prices are generally very high, but quality rooms can be had for a discounted price. It's always worth asking when you make your reservation whether any special deals are available. Most deluxe and mid-range hotels offer weekend deals throughout the year.

Need to Know

This section takes you through all the practical aspects of your trip to make it run more smoothly and to give you confidence before you go and while you are there.

Planning Ahead   162
Getting There   164
Getting Around   166
Essential Facts   168
Books and Films   171

NEED TO KNOW

Planning Ahead

WHEN TO GO

London is busy year-round, and most attractions remain open all year. Peak season is from April to September, when you should arrive with a hotel reservation and theater tickets. The quietest months are January to March and November, when hotels may give a discount.

TIME

GMT (Greenwich Mean Time) is standard. BST (British Summer Time) is 1 hour ahead (late Mar–late Oct).

TEMPERATURE

JAN	FEB	MAR	APR	MAY	JUN	JUL	AUG	SEP	OCT	NOV	DEC
42°F	45°F	50°F	55°F	63°F	68°F	72°F	72°F	66°F	57°F	50°F	45°F
6°C	7°C	10°C	13°C	17°C	20°C	22°C	22°C	19°C	14°C	10°C	7°C

Spring (March to May) has a mixture of sunshine and showers, although winter often encroaches on it.

Summer (June to August) can be unpredictable, with clear skies and hot days interspersed with rain, sultry grayness or thunderstorms.

Autumn (September to November) often has clear skies that can feel almost summery. Real autumn starts in October, and colder weather sets in during November.

Winter (December to February) is generally fairly cold, and snow can sometimes disrupt public transportation.

WHAT'S ON

January *Sales:* Shopping bargains at stores all over the city.

February *Chinese New Year:* Dragon dances and fireworks in Chinatown.

March *Chelsea Antiques Fair:* Treasures at Chelsea Old Town Hall.

April *Oxford and Cambridge Boat Race* (1st Sat): This famous annual race takes place on the Thames from Putney to Mortlake.

London Marathon: 40,000 runners zigzag through the capital.

May *Chelsea Flower Show* (end of May): One of the world's best shows takes place at the Royal Hospital, Chelsea.

June *Trooping the Colour* (2nd Sat): The "Colours" (flags) are trooped before the Queen on Horse Guards Parade, Whitehall.

Wimbledon (Jun/Jul): The world's leading grass tennis tournament.

July *BBC Proms* (Jul–Sep): Nightly world-class classical concerts in the Royal Albert Hall.

August *Notting Hill Carnival* (last Sun and Bank Holiday Monday): Europe's biggest carnival.

September *Totally Thames Festival* (all month): Arts, culture and river events along the 42-mile (67km) stretch of the Thames in London.

October *Museums at Night* (last weekend): Out of hours celebration.

BFI London Film Festival.

November *Bonfire Night* (5 Nov): Bonfires and fireworks commemorate the failed Gunpowder Plot of 1605.

Lord Mayor's Show: The City's favorite ritual, with parades and pageantry in a long procession.

December *Christmas music* (all month): Christmas music fills London's churches and many concert halls.

LONDON ONLINE

visitlondon.com
London's official site is up-to-date and comprehensive with ideas for museums, theater and restaurants, and sections for children and visitors with disabilities. It offers discounts too.

royalparks.org.uk
From Greenwich Park to Green Park, all eight of London's Royal Parks are detailed here, with information on special events and activities for children.

tfl.gov.uk
Transport for London's official site gives ideas for what to see and do, ticket information for the Underground, buses, DLR and river services. It also has a WAP-enabled journey planner.

royal.gov.uk
The official site of the British royal family, with history, royal residences, who's doing what today and a monthly online magazine.

weknowlondon.com
You can book accommodations, tickets to attractions and theaters, tours and day trips, and even order sim cards here.

londontown.com
This comprehensive site covers what's on, what's new, attractions, events, theaters, sightseeing ideas, traditions, nightlife, shopping, markets and general advice.

hrp.org.uk
This site is dedicated to London's five great historic palaces, from the Tower of London to Hampton Court Palace.

officiallondontheatre.co.uk
The Society of London Theatre's official site, with all the latest theater news, together with comprehensive interviews with stars, performance details and theater access for visitors with disabilities.

TRAVEL SITES

nationaltrust.org.uk
This independent organization owns and maintains many buildings and extensive lands, some of them in and around London.

english-heritage.org.uk/London
English Heritage is responsible for many historic sites and buildings—with ideas for days out in London.

fodors.com
A complete travel-planning site. You can research prices and weather, book air tickets, cars and rooms, pose questions (and get answers) from fellow travelers, and find links to other sites.

visitbritain.com
Great places to visit around the UK, with accommodations, transport, special offers and travel tips.

INTERNET ACCESS

All of the capital's public libraries have internet facilities. WiFi is available at airports, train stations and in the majority of cafés. Most hotels have WiFi or modem plug-in points (data ports) in rooms and public areas.

Getting There

TRAINS

● For all information, visit National Rail at nationalrail.co.uk.

● Purchase tickets at the railway station or online at thetrainline.com.

● All major London train stations are on Tube lines.

● There are eight major London train stations and sometimes a town is served by more than one (e.g. Paddington and Waterloo both serve Windsor).

● Train fares are high but deals are available if you book in advance and can be flexible about the time you travel.

NIGHT BUS

The N9 night bus, connecting Heathrow with central London (Trafalgar Square), leaves from the Central Bus Station (for Terminals 2 and 3) and Terminal 5 about every 20 minutes. The journey time is around 1 hour 15 minutes.

BY COACH

If you travel to London by long-distance coach you will probably arrive at Victoria Coach Station (VCS) on Buckingham Palace Road, which is very near Victoria train and Tube station. Alternatively, there is a taxi rank immediately outside.

AIRPORTS

Heathrow and Gatwick are the principal airports serving the city. However, Stansted, Luton and London City are increasingly busy with traffic from Continental Europe. There are train links to the Continent via Lille and Paris and road links to Channel ports.

60km (40 miles)

Luton Airport
Bus 1hr 30 min
Train 25 min

Stansted Airport
Bus 1hr 40 min
Train 40 min

London City Airport
Bus 25–40 min
DLR/Underground 25 min

Heathrow Airport
Bus approx 1hr
Train approx 15 min
Underground 1hr

Gatwick Airport
Bus 1hr 30 min–2hr 45 min
Train 30 min

FROM HEATHROW

Heathrow (heathrow.com) has four terminals (Terminals 2, 3, 4 and 5), 24km (15 miles) west of central London; all are well served by public transport. The Tube's Piccadilly line runs from 5am to 11.40pm (Terminal 4 station closes Mon–Sat 11.35pm, Sun 11.15pm) and takes about an hour. On Fridays and Saturdays there's a 24-hour service from Terminals 2 and 3 and Terminal 5. The Heathrow Express (heathrowexpress.com), a high-speed rail link to Paddington station, runs from 5.10am to around 11.40pm every 15 minutes. Prices are high for the 15-minute journey. A cheaper alternative is the Heathrow Connect local stopping service (heathrowconnect.com) to Paddington station; journey time 30–50 minutes.

National Express (nationalexpress.com) coaches run from around 4.30am to 10pm to Victoria Coach Station; the fastest journey time is around 50 minutes. Taxis wait outside the terminals; the trip takes under an hour, depending on traffic, and costs from £50 to £70.

FROM GATWICK

Gatwick airport (gatwickairport.com) is 48km (30 miles) south of central London and the best way to reach the city is by train. The Gatwick Express (gatwickexpress.com) train leaves for Victoria Station every 15 minutes, (4.35am–1.35am) and takes 30 minutes. Southern (southernrailway.com) runs slower but cheaper services to Victoria, and Thameslink (thameslinkrailway.com) goes to London Bridge and King's Cross/St. Pancras International. Taxis cost more than £100.

FROM STANSTED
Stansted airport (stanstedairport.com) is 56km (35 miles) northeast of central London. The Stansted Express (stanstedexpress.com) to Liverpool Street Station takes around 50 minutes. Several bus/coach operators run services to Liverpool Street and Victoria stations. Journey time is up to 1 hour 40 minutes. A taxi costs from £100.

FROM LUTON AIRPORT
Luton airport (london-luton.co.uk) is 53km (33 miles) north of London. There are bus links to Victoria Coach Station, taking around 1 hour 30 minutes, and East Midlands and Thameslink trains to St. Pancras International, taking from 40 minutes. Taxis cost about £80.

FROM LONDON CITY AIRPORT
City Airport (londoncityairport.com) is at Royal Albert Docks, 14km (9 miles) east of central London. Trains from London City Airport Docklands Light Railway (DLR) station feed into the Underground system. Taxis from the terminal cost around £35.

THE CHANNEL TUNNEL
Eurostar train services (eurostar.com) connect Britain to Continental Europe, and are a great way of arriving in London, or for taking trips out to Paris, Brussels and elsewhere in Europe. The journey to Brussels takes about 2 hours, Paris about 2 hours 15 minutes.

Trains depart from St. Pancras International terminal, close to King's Cross station. Eurotunnel (eurotunnel.com) is for vehicles only. Fares are lower if you reserve ahead.

Getting Around

DRIVING TIP

Driving in London is slow, parking is expensive and fines are high. Congestion charges operate from Monday to Friday, 7am–6pm, costing £11.50 a day. Do not drive in London unless you have to; use the Tube or bus instead.

VISITORS WITH DISABILITIES

London is steadily improving its facilities for visitors with disabilities, from shops and theaters to hotels and museums. Newer attractions such as Tate Modern and the London Eye are better equipped than ancient buildings such as Westminster Abbey. Check out the London Tourist Board's comprehensive website (visitlondon.com) and guide books, such as *Access in London* (published by Access Project PHSP (accessinlondon.org). Also consult Artsline (artsline.org.uk), Can Be Done (canbedone.co.uk) and Dial (scope.org.uk/dial). DisabledGo (disabledgo.com) has information on accessible places to visit in the UK with a good section on London. William Forrester, a lecturer and wheelchair user, leads tailor-made tours in the city (☎ 01483 575401).

Underground trains (known as the Tube) and buses run from around 5am to just after midnight, when service is via night buses. The Tube runs a 24-hour service on Fridays and Saturdays. The transport system is divided into zones (clearly indicated on transport maps) and you must have a ticket valid for the zone you are in.

THE UNDERGROUND (TUBE)
Eleven color-coded lines link almost 300 stations. The network also includes the Docklands Light Railway (DLR) and London Overground, which covers large parts of the city, as well as many suburban areas.

BUSES
Plan your journey using the latest copy of the Central London bus guide, available at London Transport information centers (▷ below) or at tfl.gov.uk. Bus stops are indicated by a white sign with the red Underground logo; many now have display panels with real-time arrivals information. Note that you can no longer pay cash on London buses, so you will need to buy a Travelcard or Oyster card, or use a contactless bank card.

TAXIS
Taxis that are available for rental illuminate a yellow "For Hire" sign on the roof. Hold out your hand to hail them beside the road. Drivers of official cabs will know the city well. They are obliged to follow the shortest route unless an alternative is agreed beforehand. A "black cab" (now often not black) is licensed for up to five passengers. Meter charges increase in the evenings and at weekends. Take care using minicabs, as they may have no meter and inadequate insurance. Call a black cab via Radio Taxis (tel 020 7272 0272, radiotaxis.co.uk).

TRAVEL INFORMATION CENTERS
These sell travel passes, provide Tube, train and bus route maps and information on cheap tickets, and open daily at the following stations: Heathrow terminals 2 and 3, Gatwick Airport,

Liverpool Street, Victoria, Euston, King's Cross, Paddington and Piccadilly Circus. For Transport for London services, call 0343 222 1234.

PAYING FOR TRAVEL

Travelcards, valid after 9.30am (you must pay a surcharge to use them earlier) for unlimited travel by Tube, railway, Docklands Light Railway and buses, are sold at travel information centers, railway and Tube stations, and some shops. They cover travel for one day or seven days.

Oyster pre-pay smartcards are valid for use on the Underground, DLR, bus, Thameslink and some national rail networks. Single fares are much cheaper with Oyster than cash, and the cards can be topped up with more credit. You can buy a visitor Oyster card before arriving in the UK by visiting the Transport for London website (tfl.gov.uk).

The easiest method is to use a contactless debit or credit card, or a mobile payment app on your smartphone. This works exactly like an Oyster card—simply touch the card or your phone to the card reader on the ticket barrier on entry and exit and the correct fare will automatically be deducted. If you make multiple journeys, the total cost will be capped at the cost of a Travelcard, so there is no risk of overpaying. You just have to be careful to use the same payment card for each journey.

LONDON PASS

This pass offers free entry to more than 60 top attractions and fast-track entry to save you time. It's valid for 1, 2, 3, 6 or 10 consecutive days and prices start at £62 for a one-day adult pass. See londonpass.com for details.

BOATING AND BIKING

Thames Clippers (thamesclippers.com) runs a commuter, leisure and sightseeing service aboard high-speed catamarans.

London Cycling Campaign (lcc.org.uk) can advise on biking in the capital. You can rent a bicycle from, and return it to, one of the many Santander Cycles project docking stations scattered across London (tfl.gov.uk).

TIPS

● London is huge. It may take more than an hour to reach your destination, so allow plenty of time—and plan your day to avoid crisscrossing the city.
● When buying a Travelcard, select the appropriate pass for the areas you will visit. A card covering Zones 1 and 2 is usually adequate; pay a supplement if you go outside this area.
● Use common sense when traveling alone at night, but there is no need to be unduly concerned.
● Smoking is banned on all public transportation.

FUN TOURS

Below are some ideas for quirkier ways to explore.
● London Walks (☎ 020 7624 3978, walks.com).
● Open House Architecture (☎ 020 3006 7008, open-city.org.uk).
● By water (▷ 56–57).
● London Duck Tours (☎ 020 7928 3132, londonducktours.co.uk).
● Cable car (☎ 0343 222 1234, emiratesairline.co.uk). The Emirates Air Line is a cable car across the Thames between North Greenwich and the Royal Docks. It offers easy access to the O2 Arena with great views. The rides are approximately 10 minutes each way, shorter during rush hour.

NEED TO KNOW

Essential Facts

VISAS AND TRAVEL INSURANCE

Check visa and passport requirements before traveling; see fco.gov.uk or ukinusa.fco.gov.uk. EU citizens are covered for medical expenses with an EHIC card; insurance to cover illness and theft is still strongly advised. Visitors from outside the EU should purchase adequate travel insurance.

MONEY

The pound sterling (£) is the official currency in the UK. There are bank notes in denominations of £5, £10, £20, and £50, and coins in £1 and £2 and 1, 2, 5, 20 and 50 pence.

CREDIT CARDS

● Credit cards are widely accepted. Visa and MasterCard are the most popular, followed by American Express, Diners Club and JCB. Credit cards can also be used for withdrawing cash from ATMs (though this is pricey).
● If your credit cards are lost, report each one immediately to the credit card company and, if stolen, the police as well. For your credit card company's local 24-hour emergency number, go to ukphonebook.com. It's free but you have to register.

ELECTRICITY
● Standard supply is 240V. Motor-driven equipment needs a specific frequency; in the UK it is 50 cycles per second (kHz).

EMERGENCY TELEPHONE NUMBERS
● For police, fire or ambulance, call 999 or 112 from any telephone, free of charge. The call goes directly to the emergency services. Tell the operator which street you are on and the nearest landmark, intersection or house number. You must stay by the telephone until help arrives.

MEDICAL TREATMENT
● EU nationals and citizens of some other countries with special arrangements (Australia and New Zealand) may be eligible to receive free National Health Service (NHS) medical treatment provided that they are in possession of the correct documentation (an EHIC card for EU visitors).
● All other visitors have to pay.
● If you need an ambulance call 999 on any telephone, free of charge, or 112 from most mobiles (cellphones).
● NHS hospitals with 24-hour emergency departments include: University College Hospital, 235 Euston Road, NW1, tel 020 3456 7890; St Mary's Hospital, Praed Street, W2, tel 020 3312 6666; St Thomas' Hospital, Westminster Bridge Road, SE1, tel 020 7188 7188.
● Private hospitals, with no emergency unit, include the Cromwell Hospital, 164–178 Cromwell Road, SW5, tel 020 7460 5700.
● Dental problems: Call the NHS free helpline (tel 111) to find a walk-in center. You don't need an appointment for these but the wait can be long. King's College Hospital, Denmark Hill, SE5, has an Acute Dental Care clinic for treating serious dental problems (helpdesk tel 020 3299 1919, Mon–Fri 8.30–12.30).
● Eye specialist: Moorfields Eye Hospital, City Road, EC1, tel 020 7566 2345 is for sight-threatening emergencies only. Some opticians offer same-day repairs for glasses.

● For homeopathic pharmacies, practitioners and advice, contact the British Homeopathic Association on 020 3640 5903 or visit britishhomeopathic.org.

MEDICINES
● Many drugs cannot be bought over the counter. For an NHS prescription, you pay a modest flat rate; if a private doctor prescribes, you pay the full cost. To claim charges back on insurance, keep receipts.
● Chemists that keep longer hours include: Boots Pharmacy, 44–46 Regent Street, Piccadilly Circus, W1, is open until 11pm (Sun 6.30pm), tel 020 7734 6126; Boots Pharmacy, 114 Queensway, W2, tel 020 7229 1183, is open until midnight (Sun 6pm); Zafash Pharmacy, 233 Old Brompton Road, SW5, tel 020 7373 2798, is open daily 24 hours.

OPENING HOURS
● Major attractions: Seven days a week; some open late certain days of each week.
● Shops: Generally Mon–Sat 9.30/10am–6pm; department stores until 8 or even 10pm (Selfridges, Oxford Street). Many shops open Sun 12–5/6pm; department stores have browsing time before the tills open from 11.30am. Late-night shopping (until 8pm) is on Thu in the West End and Wed in Knightsbridge.
● Banks: Mon–Fri 9.30–5; a few remain open later or open on Sat mornings. *Bureaux de change* generally have longer opening hours. ATMs are abundant.
● Post offices: Usually Mon–Fri 9–5.30, Sat 9–12.30.

NEWSPAPERS AND MAGAZINES
Newspapers include *The Financial Times*, *The Daily Telegraph*, *The Guardian*, *The Daily Mail* and *The Times*; Sunday papers include *The Sunday Times*, *Sunday Telegraph* and *The Observer*. Free papers (Mon–Fri) are *Metro* and *London Evening Standard*, which is strong on entertainment and nightlife (thisislondon. co.uk). *Time Out* (timeout. com), published weekly on Wed), lists almost everything going and is free.

TIPPING
Many restaurants add a 12.5 percent service charge. For taxis, hairdressers and other services, 10 percent is acceptable. Tips are not usual in theaters, cinemas or concert halls, or in pubs or bars (unless there is table service).

EMBASSIES	
Australian High Commission	✉ Australia House, Strand, WC2 ☎ 020 7379 4334, uk.embassy.gov.au
Canadian High Commission	✉ Canada House, Trafalgar Square, SW1 ☎ 020 7004 6000, unitedkingdom.gc.ca
New Zealand High Commission	✉ New Zealand House, 80 Haymarket, SW1 ☎ 020 7930 8422, nzembassy.com
Embassy of the US	✉ 24 Grosvenor Square, W1 ☎ 020 7499 9000, uk.usembassy.gov

MAILING A LETTER

Stamps are sold at post offices, supermarkets and some newsagents and shops. Trafalgar Square Post Office stays open late:
✉ William IV Street, WC2
🕐 Mon–Fri 8.30–6.30 (Tue from 9.15), Sat 9–5.30. Mailboxes are red.

TELEVISION

● The five most watched channels in Britain are BBC1, BBC2, ITV1, Channel 4 and Channel 5. The BBC is funded by a licence fee and there is no advertising on any BBC channels.
● Television channels available in hotel rooms will be at least the above and most likely digital terrestrial and satellite services, with a large number of channels and a wide variety of content. Programs can also be viewed on the internet and 4G cellphones.

STUDENTS

Holders of an International Student Identity Card (ISIC) will be able to obtain some good concessions on travel and entrance fees.

PHONES

● London numbers (eight digits) are prefixed with the code 020 when dialing from outside the city. To call London from abroad, dial the country code 44, then just 20, then the eight-digit number.
● Public phones accept coins, phonecards and credit cards.
● For the operator tel 100. For the international operator or to reverse charges tel 155.
● Directory enquiries: There are many options; tel 0800 953 0720 for details and prices.
● To make international calls from the UK, dial 00, then the country code (1 for the US and Canada).
● Beware of high charges on numbers that start with 084, 087 or 09.
● Numbers starting 0800 are free.
● Before departure, consult with your cell/mobile phone provider on coverage and rates.

PUBLIC HOLIDAYS

● 1 Jan; Good Fri; Easter Mon; May Day (first Mon in May); last Mon in May; last Mon in Aug; 25 Dec; 26 Dec.
● Almost all attractions and shops close Christmas Day; many close 24 Dec, 1 Jan, Good Fri and Easter Sun as well. Some shops, restaurants and attractions remain open throughout, but check.

SENSIBLE PRECAUTIONS

● Keep valuables in a hotel or bank safe box.
● Note all passport, ticket and credit card numbers, and keep separately. Carry photocopies of the key pages of your passport.
● Make sure that bags are fully closed and keep them in sight at all times—do not put them on the floor or over the back of a chair.
● Exercise caution when traveling, particularly after dark, and keep to streets that are well lit. If using a taxi, use a black cab, or ask your hotel or restaurant to book one for you.

TOURIST INFORMATION

● There are tourist information centers all over London. Check visitlondon.com for locations.

Books and Films

London's vitality, variety, glamor and squalor have always provided rich pickings for writers and filmmakers.

London is steeped in history and acclaimed historian Peter Ackroyd's books are an involving way to get beneath the city's skin. Try *London, The Concise Biography* (2012). The updated *London: A Life in Maps* by Peter Whitfield (2017) is full of intriguing facts and insights; Lucy Inglis has entertaining revelations in *Georgian London: Into the Streets* (2014) while *Literary London* by Eloise Millar and Sam Jordison (2016) reveals the stories behind the writers, from Chaucer to the modern day.

For a quirky angle on the capital, look for *Walk the Lines* (2013), in which trivia-fan Mark Mason tells how he walked the entire length of the London Underground, overground. In *Spitalfields Life* (2013), lively pen portraits chronicle daily happenings around this revitalized area of east London. *The Zoo: The Wild and Wonderful Tale of the Founding of London Zoo* by Isobel Charman (2016) is an amazing story, full of incredible Victorian characters, human and animal.

FILMS

A feel-good, real-life film, *A Street Cat Named Bob* (2016), based on James Bowen's memoir of the same name, tells of the ex-heroin addict whose life on the streets is turned around when he adopts a stray ginger cat. Together they find fame busking around Covent Garden.

Bridget Jones's Baby, the 2016 update on the first two much-loved films, is naturally rooted in the city. *The Lady in the Van* (2015), with its wonderfully eccentric main character, is also a quintessentially London film.

James Bond's latest outing in *Sceptre* (2015) is set partly in the British Intelligence building on the Thames and climaxes on Westminster Bridge. *London Town* (2016) harks back to the punk era of the 70s, while *Kids in Love* (2016) reveals the city's bohemian side. Action thriller *London Has Fallen* (2016) has scenes shot at Somerset House.

LONDON CLASSICS

Perhaps the most famous book about London is *The Diary of Samuel Pepys*, in which the observer, Pepys, recorded events from 1600 to 1669. Many of Charles Dickens' novels have London settings, including *Oliver Twist* (1837), *The Old Curiosity Shop* (1840), *Bleak House* (1853) and *Little Dorrit* (1857). In 1887, Sir Arthur Conan Doyle introduced his character Sherlock Holmes in the novel *A Study in Scarlet*. The legendary fictional detective lived at 221b Baker Street, W1. In William Thackeray's *Vanity Fair* (1847), Becky Sharp begins her adventures in Russell Square. Humorist P.G. Wodehouse, creator of the eccentric Jeeves and Wooster, based his Drones Club on several London gentlemen's clubs of the time (1920s). *84 Charing Cross Road* (1982), a memoir of warm, funny and sad letters between New Yorker Helene Hanff and London antiquarian bookseller Frank Doel during the 1940s, is a modern classic that made a memorable movie.

Index

30 St. Mary Axe (The Gherkin) 66, 89

A

accommodations 9, 152–159
airports 164–165
Albert Memorial 66, 107
Apsley House (Wellington Museum) 9, 66
architecture 4, 14, 18–19, 22–23, 48–51, 54–55
art 15, 17, 19, 21, 34–37, 50–55, 123
auction houses 125

B

Bank of England Museum 66
Banqueting House 14–15, 100, 104
bars and clubs 131–139
bed-and-breakfast 154
   see also accommodations
books 171
Borough Market 8, 66–67, 82
British Library 17, 67
British Museum 9, 16–17, 98
Buckingham Palace 4, 9, 18–19, 101, 104
buses 164, 166

C

Canary Wharf 4, 76, 113
Changing the Guard 79
Charles Dickens Museum 67
Chelsea Physic Garden 76
children 9
Chinatown 95
Chiswick House 76
churches and cathedrals
   Holy Trinity, Sloane Square 71
   St. James's, Piccadilly 9, 73, 101, 138
   St. Paul's Cathedral 4, 9, 44–45, 57, 88, 92
   Southwark Cathedral 57, 74, 82
   Westminster Abbey 62–63, 100, 105
Churchill War Rooms 67–68, 100
cinemas 133, 134, 135
City Hall 68, 82
Clarence House 9, 68, 101
Cleopatra's Needle 68
climate 162
Courtauld Gallery 51, 94, 98
Covent Garden Piazza 68, 95

Covent Garden to Regent's Park 94–99
credit cards 168
Crossrail 165
Cutty Sark 20, 112
cycling 167

D

Design Museum 69
disabilities, visitors with 166
Docklands 4, 6, 77
driving in London 166
Dulwich Picture Gallery 76

E

East End 6–7
eating out 8, 41, 126, 142
   see also restaurants
electricity 168
embassies 169
emergencies 168
entertainment 9, 128–139
Eros 69
etiquette 142, 169
events and festivals 162
excursions
   Hampton Court Palace 78
   Windsor 79
   see also tours

F

films 171
Fleet Street to the Tower 88–93
Foundling Museum 69
Farther Afield 112–117

G

Garden Museum 69
The Gherkin (30 St. Mary Axe) 66, 89
Golden Hinde II 69–70, 83
Green Park 8, 70
Greenwich 8, 20–21, 57, 112–117
Guildhall Art Gallery 70, 88

H

Ham House 76
Hampstead Heath 8, 77
Hampton Court Palace 78
Handel & Hendrix in London 9, 70
Hayward Gallery 70–71
history 6, 10–11, 14–15, 22–23, 58–59, 62–63
HMS *Belfast* 71, 82
Holy Trinity, Sloane Square 71
hotels 9, 154–159
houses see palaces

Houses of Parliament 22–23, 56, 100, 104
Hyde Park 8, 71, 106–111

I

Imperial War Museum 24–25, 86
internet access 163

J

Jewish Museum 77

K

Kensington Gardens 8, 26, 27, 107, 110
Kensington Palace 26–27, 107, 110
Kenwood House 8, 77
Kew Gardens 8, 77
Knightsbridge 28–29, 110

L

Leadenhall Building 71
libraries 17, 67
London Eye 30–31, 56, 83, 86
London Transport Museum 71–72
London Underground 5, 166
London Wetland Centre 77
lost/stolen property 165

M

Madame Tussauds 72
mail 170
maps 84–85, 90–91, 96–97, 102–103, 108–109, 114–115
medical treatment 168–169
Millennium Footbridge 4, 57
money 168
museums and galleries
   Apsley House (Wellington Museum) 9, 66
   Bank of England Museum 66
   British Museum 9, 16–17, 98
   Charles Dickens Museum 67
   Churchill War Rooms 67–68, 100
   Courtauld Gallery 51, 94, 98
   Design Museum 69
   Dulwich Picture Gallery 76
   Foundling Museum 69
   Garden Museum 69
   Guildhall Art Gallery 70, 88
   Handel & Hendrix in London 9, 70
   Hayward Gallery 70–71
   Imperial War Museum 24–25, 86
   Jewish Museum 77

London Transport Museum 71–72
Museum of London 32–33, 88, 92
Museum of London Docklands 77
National Gallery 34–35, 100, 104
National Maritime Museum 21, 112
National Portrait Gallery 36–37, 100, 104
Natural History Museum 38–39, 106, 110
Petrie Museum 72
Photographers' Gallery 72
Queen's Gallery 19
Royal Academy of Arts 73
Science Museum 9, 46–47, 106, 110
Sir John Soane's Museum 9, 74, 94
Somerset House 50–51, 94, 98
Tate Britain 52–53, 104
Tate Modern 4, 8, 54–55, 83, 86
Victoria and Albert Museum 60–61, 106, 110
V&A Museum of Childhood 77
Wallace Collection 75
Whitechapel Art Gallery 77
music venues 133–139

N
National Gallery 34–35, 100, 104
National Maritime Museum 21, 112
National Portrait Gallery 36–37, 100, 104
Natural History Museum 38–39, 106, 110
newspapers and magazines 169
nightlife see entertainment

O
Old Royal Naval College 20, 112
Olympic Games 4, 11
opening hours 169

P
palaces and houses
Banqueting House 14–15, 100, 104
Buckingham Palace 4, 9, 18–19, 101, 104
Chiswick House 76

Clarence House 9, 68, 101
Ham House 76
Hampton Court Palace 78
Kensington Palace 26–27, 107, 110
Kenwood House 8, 77
St. James's Palace 18, 42, 101
Somerset House 50–51, 94, 98
Spencer House 74–75
Windsor 63, 79
parks and gardens 8, 9, 20, 26, 27, 42–43, 70, 71, 73, 76, 77, 100, 104, 107, 110, 113, 116
personal safety 170
Peter Pan statue 27, 72
Petrie Museum 72
Photographers' Gallery 72
population 4
Portobello Road Market 40–41, 116
public holidays 170

Q
Queen Elizabeth II 11, 18–19, 79
Queen's House 20–21, 112

R
Regent's Park 8, 9, 73, 94
restaurants 8, 140–151
Royal Academy of Arts 73
Royal Family 10–11, 18–19, 26–27, 63, 68, 101
Royal Observatory 21, 113

S
St. James's Palace 18, 42, 101
St. James's Park 42–43, 100, 104
St. James's, Piccadilly 9, 73, 101, 138
St. Katharine Docks 73, 89
St. Paul's Cathedral 4, 9, 44–45, 88, 92
Science Museum 9, 46–47, 106, 110
SEA LIFE London Aquarium 74
Shakespeare's Globe 48–49, 83, 86, 139
The Shard 74, 82
shopping 7, 8, 28–29, 40–41, 66–67, 68, 110, 118–127
Sir John Soane's Museum 9, 74, 94
Soho 95
Somerset House 50–51, 94, 98
South Bank 4, 30, 82–87

South Kensington 17
Southwark Cathedral 57, 74, 82
Spencer House 74–75
students 170

T
Tate Britain 52–53, 104
Tate Modern 4, 8, 54–55, 83, 86
taxis 166
telephones 170
television 170
temperatures 162
Temple of Mithras 75, 89
Thames river cruise 56–57, 101, 104
theaters 133–139
time 162
timeline 10–11
tipping 147, 169
tourist information 163, 167, 170
tours
Around Hyde Park 106–111
Covent Garden to Regent's Park 94–99
Fleet Street to the Tower 88–93
Farther Afield 112–117
South Bank 82–87
Westminster and St. James's 100–105
see also excursions
Tower of London 4, 57, 58–59, 89, 92
Trafalgar Square 75, 100
transport 4–5, 164–167
travel insurance 168
travel passes 167
travel planning 162–170
Tube, the 5, 166

V
Victoria and Albert Museum 60–61, 106, 110
V&A Museum of Childhood 77
visas 168

W
Wallace Collection 75
websites 163
Westminster Abbey 62–63, 100, 105
Westminster and St. James's 100–105
Whitechapel Art Gallery 77
Windsor 63, 79

Z
ZSL London Zoo 75

The Automobile Association would like to thank the following photographers, companies and picture libraries for their assistance in the preparation of this book

2i AA/S. Montgomery; 2ii AA/N. Setchfield; 2iii AA/J. Tims; 2iv AA/S. Montgomery; 2v; AA/J. Tims; 3i AA/J. Tims; 3ii AA/J. Tims; 3iii AA/R. Mort; 3iv AA/S. Montgomery; 4tl AA/S.; Montgomery; 5 AA/J. Tims; 6c Benjamin John/Alamy Stock Photo; 6/7t GeoPic/Alamy Stock Photo; 6/7tc Kathy deWitt/; Alamy Stock Photo; 6/7b Stuart Forster/Alamy Stock Photo; 7c Bombaert Patrick/Alamy Stock Photo; 8/9i AA/J. Tims; 8/9ii; AA/J. Tims; 8/9iii AA/J. Tims; 8/9iv AA/N. Setchfield; 8/9v AA/J. Tims; 8/9vi AA/N. Setchfield; 10bl AA/J. Tims; 10br The Art Archive/Alamy Stock Photo; 11bl Mary Evans Picture Library/Alamy Stock Photo; 11br; AA/J. Tims; 12 AA/N. Setchfield; 14tl AA/J. Tims; 14tr AA/S. Montgomery; 14cr/15c AA/J. Tims; 15tl AA/J. Tims; 16t AA/J. Tims; 17tl AA/N. Setchfield; 17tr AA/J. Tims; 17c AA/J. Tims; 18t/19tl; AA/J. Tims; 19tc AA/S. Montgomery; 19tr Courtesy Royal Collection 2011, Her Majesty Queen; Elizabeth II/Derry Moore; 19c Monica Wells/TTL; 20t AA/N. Setchfield; 21tl AA/AA; 21cl AA/S; and O Mathews; 21c AA/N. Setchfield; 22t/23tl AA/J. Tims; 22c/23cl AA/J. Tims; 23c AA/J.; Tims; 23tr AA/J. Tims; 24/25 AA/J. Tims; 25tl AA/J. Tims; 25tr AA/J. Tims; 25c AA/J. Tims; 26; London Stills; 27tl AA/J. Tims; 27tr AA/S. Montgomery; 27cl London Stills; 27cr AA/J. Tims; 28; Courtesy Harvey Nichols; 29tl Courtesy Swarovski/Yellow Door; 29tr Travelshots.com/Alamy Stock Photo; 29cl Courtesy Harvey Nichols; 29cr AA/S. Montgomery; 30 Courtesy EDF Energy London Eye/; British Tourist Authority/James McCormick; 31tl Courtesy EDF Energy London Eye; 31tr Courtesy; EDF Energy London Eye; 31c Courtesy EDF Energy London Eye; 32/33bl AA/J. Tims; 33tr AA/J. Tims; 33cr AA/J. Tims; 34/35 Ronald Weir/TTL; 35tl AA/J. Tims; 35cl; AA/J. Tims; 35c AA/J. Tims; 35tr Courtesy The National Gallery; 36 Courtesy The National Portrait; Gallery; 37tl Courtesy The National Portrait Gallery/Andrew Putler; 37tr AA/J. Tims; 37cl; AA/S. Montgomery; 37cr AA/J. Tims; 38l AA/N. Setchfield; 38tr/39tl AA/M. Jourdan; 38cr/39cl; Courtesy Natural History Museum; 39tr Courtesy Natural History Museum/D. Adams; 40/41; Pawel Libera Images/Alamy Stock Photo; 41tr London Stills; 41cr AA/M. Jourdan; 42 David Noton/TTL; 43tl; AA; 43tr SJ Images/Alamy Stock Photo 44l London Stills 44tr/45tl Courtesy St Paul's Cathedral/Peter Smith; 44br AA/AA; 45bl AA/AA; 45r AA/S. Montgomery; 46l Courtesy Science Museum; 46tr/47tl; AA/J. Tims; 46br/47bl AA/J. Tims; 47r Courtesy Science Museum; 48l AA/R. Turpin; 48/49; James Barrett/Alamy Stock Photo; 50tl AA/J. Tims; 50tr/51tl The Courtauld Gallery/J. Tims; 50cr/51cl AA/J.; Tims; 51tr The Courtauld Gallery/J. Tims; 52t AA/S. Montgomery; 53tl AA/S. Montgomery; 53cl AA/S. Montgomery; 53tr AA/S. Montgomery; 54tl AA/N. Setchfield; 54tr/55tl AA/J. Tims; 54cr AA/S. Montgomery; 55cl AA/S. Montgomery; 55tr Switch House, Tate Modern © Iwan Baan; 56t/57tl AA/C. Sawyer; 56cl AA/T. Woodcock; 56cr/57cl AA/J. Tims; 57tr Courtesy; London Duck Tours Ltd; 57cr AA/J. Tims; 58t AA/S. Montgomery; 59tl AA/S. Montgomery; 59tr; AA/S. Montgomery; 59c AA/S. Montgomery; 60t/61tl Maurice Crooks/Alamy Stock Photo; 61tr Courtesy; Victoria and Albert Museum/Alan Williams; 61cr Courtesy Victoria and Albert Museum/R.; Waite; 62tl Tom Mackie/TTL; 62tr AA/J. Tims; 62cr/63cl AA/J. Tims; 63tl AA/J. Tims; 63tr AA/J.; Tims; 64t AA/R. Mort; 66bl AA/J. Tims; 66br AA/S. Montgomery; 67bl AA/J. Tims; 67br AA/J.; Tims; 68b AA/N. Setchfield; 69bl AA/J. Tims; 69br AA/J. Tims; 70b AA/S. McBride; 71b AA/N.; Setchfield; 72bl AA/J. Tims; 72br AA/J. Tims; 73bl AA/S. Montgomery; 73br Marcin Rogozinski/Alamy Stock Photo; 74bl AA/S. Montgomery; 74br Sir John Soane's Museum/Photo Gareth Gardner; 75b AA/J. Tims; 76bl AA/P.; Kenward; 76br Courtesy Museum of London; 78bl AA/D. Forss; 78br AA/D. Forss; 79bl AA/W.; Voysey; 79br AA/J. Tims; 80 AA/S. Montgomery; 82tr AA/J. Tims; 82cl AA/S. Montgomery; 82br AA/M. Jourdan; 83tr AA/S. Montgomery; 83cl AA/R. Turpin; 83br Courtesy EDF Energy; London Eye; 86i AA/J. Tims; 86ii AA/J. Tims; 86iii AA/S. Montgomery; 86iv AA/S. Montgomery; 87 AA/J. Tims; 88tr AA/N. Setchfield; 89tr AA/S. Montgomery; 89 lower c AA/W. Voysey; 92tr Courtesy Museum of London; 92cr Courtesy St Paul's Cathedral/Peter Smith; 92br AA/S.; Montgomery; 93b AA/J. Tims; 94l N. Setchfield/Alamy Stock Photo; 94b The Courtauld Gallery/J. Tims; 95tr AA/J. Tims; 95br AA/J. Tims; 98tr AA/N. Setchfield; 98br The Courtauld Gallery/J. Tims; 100t Courtesy The National Portrait Gallery/Andrew Putler; 100cr AA/J. Tims; 101t London; Stills; 101bl AA/C. Sawyer 104i AA/J. Tims; 104ii AA/S. Montgomery; 104iii AA/J. Tims; 104iv; London Stills; 104v AA/S. Montgomery; 104vi AA/S. Montgomery; 104vii AA/S. Montgomery; 104viii AA/N. Setchfield; 105tr AA/B. Smith; 106l Courtesy Victoria and Albert Museum; 107tr AA/J. Tims; 107b AA/S. Montgomery; 110i AA/P. Kenward; 110ii AA/P. Kenward; 110iii; AA/T. Woodcock; 110iv AA/J. Tims; 110v Courtesy Victoria and Albert Museum/Morley von; Sternberg; 112tr AA/S and O Mathews; 112br David Noton/TTL; 113t AA/S and O Mathews; 113cl AA/W. Voysey; 116tr Rik Hamilton/Alamy Stock Photo; 116cr AA/M. Jourdan; 118 AA/J. Tims; 120/121i AA/S. Montgomery; 120/121ii AA/P. Kenward; 120/121iii AA/R. Turpin; 120/121iv AA/N. Strange; 120/121v AA/M. Trelawny; 120/121vi AA/S. Montgomery; 125br AA/J. Tims; 127br AA/S.; Montgomery; 128 AA/J. Tims; 130/131i AA/J. Tims; 130/131ii AA/J. Tims; 130/131iii AA/M.; Jourdan; 130/131iv AA/S. Montgomery; 130/131v AA/J. Tims; 134 AA/S. Montgomery; 139 Brian Anthony/Alamy Stock Photo; 140 AA/J. Tims; 142ri AA/AA; 142ii AA/M. Jourdan; 142iii AA/N. Setchfield 142iv AA/J.; Tims; 146bl AA/N. Setchfield; 146br AA/J. Tims; 148 AA/N. Setchfield 152 AA/R. Mort; 154i; AA/W. Voysey; 154ii AA/J. Tims; 154iii OneOff Travel/Alamy Stock Photo; 154iv VIEW Pictures Ltd/Alamy Stock Photo; 157 AA/S. Montgomery; 158 AA/J. Tims; 160 AA/S. Montgomery.

London 25 Best

WRITTEN BY Louise Nicholson
ADDITIONAL WRITING BY Sue Dobson
UPDATED BY Sue Dobson
SERIES EDITOR Clare Ashton
COVER DESIGN Chie Ushio, Yuko Inagaki
DESIGN WORK Liz Baldin
IMAGE RETOUCHING AND REPRO Ian Little

Published in the United Kingdom by AA Publishing

ISBN 978-0-1475-4713-2

THIRTEENTH EDITION

SPECIAL SALES
This book is available for special discounts for bulk purchases for sales promotions or premiums. For more information, email specialmarkets@penguinrandomhouse.com.

Color separation by AA Digital Department
Printed and bound by Leo Paper Products, China

10 9 8 7 6 5 4 3 2 1

A05522
Mapping © Crown copyright and database rights 2017 Ordnance Survey. 100021153.

Titles in the Series

- Amsterdam
- Bangkok
- Barcelona
- Boston
- Brussels and Bruges
- Budapest
- Chicago
- Dubai
- Dublin
- Edinburgh
- Florence
- Hong Kong
- Istanbul
- Krakow
- Las Vegas
- Lisbon
- London
- Madrid
- Melbourne
- Milan
- Montréal
- Munich
- New York City
- Orlando
- Paris
- Rome
- San Francisco
- Seattle
- Shanghai
- Singapore
- Sydney
- Tokyo
- Toronto
- Venice
- Vienna
- Washington, D.C.